1. The Springs of Carmel

The Springs of Carmel

The Springs of Carmel

An introduction to Carmelite spirituality

Peter Slattery

ALBA · HOUSE   NEW · YORK

SOCIETY OF ST. PAUL. 2187 VICTORY BLVD. STATEN ISLAND. NEW YORK 10314

Alba
House

Library of Congress Cataloging-in-Publication Data

Slattery, Peter.
    The springs of Carmel : an introduction to Carmelite spirituality
/ Peter Slattery.
       p. cm.
    Includes bibliographical references.
    ISBN 0-8189-0604-9
    1. Carmelites—Spiritual life.   2. Spirituality—Catholic Church
—History.   3. Catholic Church—Doctrines—History.   I. Title.
BX3203.S52   1991   91-17926
248—dc20   CIP

Produced and designed in the United States of America by the
Fathers and Brothers of the Society of St. Paul,
2187 Victory Boulevard, Staten Island, New York 10314-6603,
as part of their communications apostolate.

ISBN: 0-8189-0604-9

Printing Information:

Current Printing - first digit   5   6   7   8   9   10

Year of Current Printing - first year shown

        2005   2006   2007   2008   2009   2010   2011   2012

Acknowledgments

Extracts from the following titles: _The Collected Works of St. Teresa, The Collected Works of St. John of the Cross_, both translated by K. Kavanaugh, OCD and O. Rodriguez, OCD, _The Story of a Soul_ translated by J. Clarke, OCD, used with permission from ICS Publications, Washington, DC, USA.

The Rule of St. Albert from translation of Bede Edwards, OCD in _Rule of St. Albert_ used with permission of the Society of the Little Flower, Darien, IL, USA.

Extracts from G. Gutierrez' _A Theology of Liberation_ (15th anniversary edition), used with permission from Orbis Books, New York, USA and SCM Press, London, UK.

Extracts from _Doctrine and Life_ XXIV (Jan. 1974) on: "The Paradox of Prayers" by Noel-Dermott O'Donoghue, OCD, used with permission from Dominican Publications, Dublin, UK.

Extracts from _General Correspondence_ Vols. 1 & 2, translated by J. Clarke, OCD, used with permission from ICS Publications, Washington, DC, USA.

Contents

Introduction

Over the years I have often been asked by people to give an explanation of Carmelite spirituality. It has been difficult to recommend any book in English. There are commentaries on the spirituality of the great Carmelite saints, St. Teresa of Avila, St. John of the Cross and St. Thérèse of Lisieux. However, I have never found a straight forward and succinct explanation of the Carmelite tradition from its foundations until the present day.

This book is an attempt to bring together the charism and tradition of Carmel, that charism which has inspired men and women, religious and lay, for nearly eight centuries.

Carmelite spirituality has something to say to the women and men of today, because it leads them to love and freedom. In following in the footsteps of Jesus in faith, people will find not only a mystical love, but an asceticism of love, or, in other words, a passion for God and for life.

Carmelites propose to people two models for this way of love and freedom — Elijah, the prophet, and Mary, the Mother of Jesus. These are the inspirers of the Carmelite way of life which has a strong message for people of countries of the north and south, and east and west. The centrality of Christ teaches people how to love in their daily life and equips them not only with a discipline, or an asceticism, but transports them to a contemplative love of God and his creation. This life of love gives people an experience of inner freedom or liberation, by which they can work in their milieu to bring freedom and love to others. So Carmelites see their spirituality as not simply something from the middle ages or from 16th century Spain, but as an extremely relevant gift for today's world.

The Carmelites originated on Mount Carmel in Palestine as a small group of Latin hermits. They were organized under a prior, or leader, by the Patriarch of Jerusalem when he gave them the Rule of St. Albert between 1206 and 1214. They moved to Europe after the Holy Land fell to the Saracens, and were included among the mendicant friars like the Franciscans, Dominicans and Augustinians. In fact in England, Scotland and Ireland, because of their white cloak, they were nicknamed the White Friars. During the middle ages they were well known throughout Europe, and produced saints, theologians, artists, poets, and politicians. A female branch of the order developed slowly, but by 1415 was approved by Blessed John Soreth.

During the counter reformation, St. Teresa of Avila wanted the order to return to the simplicity of the Rule of St. Albert. She founded convents of nuns, and, with the help of St. John of the Cross, monasteries of friars, who wanted to live much like the original hermits on Mount Carmel. These two great Spanish Mystics, through their lives and writings, developed the heritage they received from the medieval Carmelites, and articulated the classical expression of Carmelite spirituality.

From the 16th century until the present day the Carmelite nuns and friars lived in two orders, the Carmelites and the discalced Carmelites. In the last two hundred years, many orders of sisters, one of priests, and several secular institutes have taken the Carmelite charism as the foundation of their congregations. In fact, today some 50,000 religious profess the Rule of St. Albert and follow the Carmelite way of life. Through the Scapular confraternity, and groups of Third Order Carmelites, the spirit of the order has spread far beyond the nuns and the friars. Thus, today one can say there is a true Carmelite family which takes its inspiration from Mount Carmel and all that it implies.

Because there have been in many parts of the world a considerable renewed interest in prayer, contemplation, mysticism and things of the spirit, there has been a resurgence of interest in Carmelite spirituality. In several parts of the world there have been many who have been turning away from the purely rational and material, and are beginning to seek oases of the spirit in their daily lives. This book will help them as an introduction to the mystical and contemplative traditions of Carmel. Another sign of renewed interest in Carmelite spirituality is that during the reign of Pope John Paul II seven Carmelites have been beatified.

In this book, we will explore Carmelite spirituality through two main ways — first, the people of Carmel and second, the images, the metaphors and symbols of Carmel. In this way we shall be able to look into the soul and heart of Carmel and find encouragement for ourselves today.

As regards the people of Carmel we will look at the Rule of Albert, Elijah the Prophet, Mary the Mother of Jesus, St. Teresa of Avila, St. John of the Cross, St. Thérèse of Lisieux, Blessed Titus Brandsma and Blessed Edith Stein. Out of all the people and saints of Carmel, these will help us to plumb the depths of Carmel. The beauty and simplicity of the Rule of St. Albert is basic to Carmelites; Elijah and Mary were the original inspirers of the first hermits; St. Teresa and St. John of the Cross, the great exponents of the charism, and St. Thérèse, Blessed Edith Stein and Blessed Titus are Carmelites applicable to 20th century men and women. There will be also an attempt to choose people from the foundation of the tradition, some from the classical periods of the tradition, and some from our own time. The choice will be influenced by an attempt to balance the masculine and feminine influences of the tradition.

The chapters of the book will also explore the dominant images, metaphors and symbols which the people of Carmel have used.

Chapter 1 will deal with the Rule of Albert, given to a group of men who saw themselves as hermits, pilgrims and later mendicants. An exploration of these three words gives great insight into how the first Carmelites understood the meaning of their lives. This also helps to explain the brevity, simplicity, originality, profundity and power of the Rule of St. Albert.

Chapter 2 will explore how and why the first Carmelites took the Prophet Elijah as an inspiration. The whole force of prophecy in the Hebrew scriptures, and the contribution of Elijah, will help explain the hermits of Mount Carmel. This will also help us to understand why Carmelites look on Elijah as a model for the order and why modern Carmelites stress this prophetic element of the charism of the order.

Chapter 3 will look at Carmel and Mary. From the very beginning Carmelites dedicated themselves to Mary, and in fact the official title of the order is "The Brothers of the Blessed Virgin Mary of Mount Carmel." Mary is both Virgin and Mother and these images add insight to the charism and spirit of the order.

Chapter 4 will look at the life and writings of St. Teresa of Avila. Her writings reveal the images and metaphors which have become classics in the whole of western spirituality. The castle, the waters, the journey, all help to plumb the depths of the soul of Carmel.

Chapter 5 will introduce St. John of the Cross. He is one of the great mystics of all time, and one of the great poets of the Spanish language. He used metaphors of love and ecstasy, of night and darkness, of the journey up the Mount of Carmel, all of which help to explain the heart of Carmel.

Chapter 6 will look at the life of St. Thérèse of Lisieux. The little way, simplicity, humility and the metaphors of desert, childhood and flower have inspired millions of men and women in this century.

Chapter 7 will introduce Blessed Titus Brandsma, a Carmelite friar, murdered by the Nazis in Dachau in World War II. As prophet, academic, writer, lecturer and administrator he has left a legacy to the Carmelite tradition. As martyr, he has inspired many men and women, both Carmelites and others, to withstand injustice, oppression and alienation where they see it in today's world.

Chapter 8 will show how Edith Stein brings the Carmelite tradition into the hopes and tragedies of the 20th century. For her the symbol of the Cross helps to explain the horrors of the Jewish holocaust and, indeed, her own martyrdom in the gas chambers of Auschwitz.

Chapter 9 will draw these people and their metaphors together so that we can articulate Carmelite spirituality today. We will look at Carmelites who pray, struggle and work for peace and justice in all parts of the world. Nuns, friars, religious sisters and lay men and women, who are inspired by Carmelite spirituality, not only carry on the traditions of the past, but re-interpret for the Church the heart, soul and mind of Carmel.

Once we have the images, we can then begin reflecting upon them so that we might grow in understanding and insight. The images lead us more profoundly into our experience, and enable us to enter into the meaning of our lives. Our experience produces feelings; the feelings reveal images; they lead to understanding and deeper appreciation of our spiritual life. We can use our active imagination to help us plumb the depth of our symbols — those we use in our own life and associations. For example, St. Benedict called the monastery a school, St. Ignatius saw the spiritual life like doing exercises. This process has the potential for deepening our awareness of our spiritual journey and that of our community.

For reflection: individuals or groups

1. *What metaphors, images and symbols do you use when writing or speaking about your spiritual experience? Do you use images like "journey," "spring," "mountain," etc.?*

Suggestions for writing and sharing

1. *Before you share with anyone, write down how you use your images, and notice, as you write, how you relate them to other images. In an unstructured way of writing, you may notice past experiences both joyful and painful may surface.*

2. *Does your writing bring up some images which you had not noticed you used very much when writing about your spiritual life?*

3. *When you are ready to share with a spiritual friend or colleague, share only that which you feel free and comfortable sharing.*

The Springs of Carmel

Chapter 1

Mount Carmel and the Rule of St. Albert

The Carmelite order professes none of the classical rules (St. Basil, St. Benedict, St. Augustine), but rather a rule or form of life unique to itself. This rule is called the Rule of St. Albert, and was given to the hermits of Mount Carmel about the years 1206 to 1214.

The Carmelites began on Mount Carmel in the Holy Land near the city of Haifa. A group of hermits lived near a spring called the spring of Elijah. There was not one charismatic person who could be called the founder of the order. The Carmelites did not have a Dominic or Francis-like figure, which fact caused them a great deal of trouble in the middle ages.

The place where the first Carmelites lived is near a spring called, from ancient times, the Spring of Elijah. In Israel today there is a gully on Mount Carmel known as Wadi'aijn-es-Siah, three kilometers from the summit overlooking the sea. Here modern archeologists have found ruins of a monastery which dates back to the time of the crusades.

From time immemorial, Mount Carmel has been a holy place, and today is holy not only to Carmelites, but to all Christians, to Jews and to Moslems. Therefore, it is not surprising that some people wanted to stay on Mount Carmel and live a life of prayer after making their pilgrimage, or fighting their crusade to free the Holy Land for Christian pilgrims.

The short and unique rule of St. Albert can be better understood when we investigate the concept of hermit and pilgrim held by people of the middle ages. The first group of Carmelites was living a prayerful life before they got their rule from St. Albert.

Hermit

A hermit is a holy person, living alone, wanting to follow Christ more fully. However, during the 11th and 12th centuries, the period of interest to us, the term was analogous and rather equivocal. In our period, it was used often as a reaction to the monasticism of the day, which was closely integrated into the feudal system of Europe. So very often the hermit was an alternative lifestyle Christian, who wished not only to follow Christ more fully, but to live a simple life apart from the towns or monasteries. Because the monasteries had so much to do with the temporal society of the period, the monks were forced to devote much of their time to temporal administrative duties. The hermits sought a more simple life, a more effective poverty and freedom from the busy life of the monasteries. Expressions such as hermitage, hermit, solitude, solitary life came into favor.

However, these terms did not always mean the same thing. Some monasteries allowed either their monks to live a solitary life, or encouraged groups of hermits to live under the guidance and protection of the Abbot. One kind of hermit could follow the solitary life of an anchorite, another could live with a group of hermits like a cenobite, and yet another could embrace the life of an anchorite dependent on a nearby monastery.

During the 11th and 12th centuries, there appeared

hermits among lay people, who reacted against all known forms of religious life. For them the rules of the orders, like St. Augustine or St. Benedict, would not allow them to live a simple gospel life. These new groups of lay hermits lacked organization and were sometimes condemned by local bishops or abbots. Their common characteristic was that they were reacting against the monasteries, their wealth, their close connection with secular life, their power both temporal and ecclesiastical. They wanted to live the poverty of Christ, by fasting, praying and living in extremely simple dwellings, and moving around on continual pilgrimage.

In spite of this the life of the monk was stricter as regards stability to one place, and obedience to the Abbot. Hermits were considered to be living not only on the fringes of secular society, but on the edge of Church life. They were often suspect as regards their orthodoxy, and were thought of on the lowest step on the ladder to religious perfection.

However, there appeared other groups of hermits who thought that their position in the Church was quite anomolous as long as they were without a rule. Many accepted the Rule of St. Augustine and they became the nucleus in the 1250's of the Augustinian hermits, later the friars. Again others accepted the Rule of St. Benedict. This unease seems to have been the reason why the hermits on Mount Carmel went to Albert, the Patriarch of Jerusalem, to ask for a rule. What made them different and interesting was that they did not accept an existing rule, and in the future would cling to the Rule of St. Albert, even though to adopt another probably would have solved many of their problems. Obviously, for the early hermits on Mount Carmel the Rule of St. Albert was a source of their group identity.

Pilgrim

The condition of a pilgrim was very popular in the ascetical life of the medieval Church. In the Church of the 12th century pilgrims were not only people who went to centers of devotion, but pilgrimage was a state of mind. To be in the state of a pilgrim, one had to be a stranger to this world, not have a stable home, and be always on the move. To set forth as a pilgrim meant to abandon one's familiar environment, in order to live in a place where one was not known, to be a foreigner without family or friends, without power or security. It was a form of exile, or abandonment, a form of conversion and doing penance.

In leaving one's own home, pilgrims lived in a region where they were unknown, where they enjoyed no civil rights, lacked power and influence and were completely on the margin. In this sense they were poor and powerless, like Christ, following the naked Christ as a naked disciple.

Pilgrimage, then, was a search for solitude, a form of the solitary life. Thus many hermits were itinerants. It was an abandonment which was often the object of a vow. Sometimes the local church consecrated the pilgrim with a blessing, a special habit and a pilgrim's staff.

Many pilgrims not only sought a powerless and solitary life, but traveled to a holy place to pray, minister to other pilgrims, and care for the poor and the sick. The ultimate holy place for the medieval pilgrim was the Holy Land, seen as the patrimony of Christ.

In the pilgrimage to Jerusalem, these images and ascetical values were found in an eminent degree — a break with the world, with one's homeland, a journey to one's true homeland, and a liberation of oneself from all the bonds of this life.

Often the pilgrim to the Holy Land vowed to stay there forever. The fact of being in the Holy Land was seen as dedicating one's life more closely to Christ. In feudal terms one became a liege-man of Christ the King, a vassal in the following of Christ, to whom one owed absolute allegiance.

In this sense many of those who became ascetical pilgrims were lay-hermits who were free from vows of obedience and stability in the established orders of the time.

A pilgrim was a penitent who set out on a trip to perform voluntary or imposed penance. Another form of pilgrimage was that of a crusader, including military activity with risk of life for the love of Christ and in remission of sin. A hermit was a penitent who more or less adopted a stable abode.

Rule of St. Albert

Consequently, a group of these pilgrim-hermits lived on Mount Carmel near the Wadi'aijn-es-Siah sometimes after 1191, after the Treaty of Hattin. They asked the Patriarch of Jerusalem for a rule of life. It is highly significant that Albert of Vercelli did not simply give them one of the rules in existence — St. Basil, St. Benedict or St. Augustine. But he gave them a simple formula of life, sometime between 1206 and 1214. Albert was murdered at Acre in 1214, and is venerated as a saint, in the Carmelite order, with a feast on 17 September.

The rule of St. Albert imitated the style of New Testament letters and included references to the early Fathers of the Church, which was fairly standard for curial documents of the period. So, while the rule supported a new way of life, it was in continuity with the Gospels and the great traditions of early religious life and the Desert Fathers.

Initially, the rule was written in the form of a letter without divisions into chapters. Now it has an introduction, 18 short chapters and a conclusion. The titles given to these chapters reflect a later understanding of the rule, and do not seem to correspond to the original purpose of the letter. The rule has

almost 100 quotations and allusions to Scripture, which reveals
great fidelity to, and familiarity with, the Bible.

> (*The Rule of St. Albert appears as an appendix at the end of
> this chapter.*)

Recent research on the Rule of St. Albert organizes the text
as follows:[1]

1. **Introduction:** The introduction encourages a gospel way of
   life which is Christocentric and paschal.

2. **Chapters 1 to 6:** These chapters present an infrastructure
   for living out these ideals.

3. **Chapters 7 to 11:** These chapters concretize the ideal
   presented in the introduction, describe the manner of living
   in community, and the foundations for this community.

4. **Chapters 12 to 18:** These chapters describe the means
   necessary to attain the proposed ideal.

5. **Conclusion:** The conclusion calls for fidelity and discernment in living out this norm of life.

Commentary on the Rule

Before taking each section of the rule in detail it may be
well to deal with the overall nucleus of the rule first. The Rule of
St. Albert describes a community striving to reproduce in its
own life the model of the first Christian community as in Acts

---

1 This research has been summarized by Secondin, B., O.Carm., "Carmelite Fraternity and
Christian Community: The Rule of Carmel between Past and Present," in *Nubecula*, 36, 2 & 3,
(1985), pp. 1-44.

2:4. The rule gives the structures to achieve this life-plan and the means for continual and ongoing conversion. The rule is fundamentally Christocentric — and, thus, all Carmelite spirituality is founded on it. This theme of the centrality of the resurrection of Christ runs through the Institution, an inspirational document for medieval Carmelites, St. Teresa, St. John of the Cross, St. Thérèse and Blessed Titus Brandsma, and, indeed, much of 20th century Carmelite literature.

1. Introduction: St. Albert's greeting is taken from Scripture and presents the rule as a contemporary living out of the word of God.[2] The rule states that there are multiple forms of the religious life, but this rule gives Carmelites a characteristic way of following Christ. This way is shown to be in continuity with tradition and the holy Fathers who gave birth to religious life.

2. Chapters 1 to 6: What are the conditions needed in order to live out this ideal? Chapters 1 to 6 indicate some of these. For example, the first chapter was somewhat innovative when it called for a prior and not an abbot to lead the community. The relationship of the abbot toward his subjects is a vertical relationship, one of father to children. The relationship of the prior to his subjects, on the other hand, is horizontal, between brothers or equals. The prior, as is evident later in the rule, is chosen to serve. The Carmelite order was born and remains participatory in its organization and decentralized.

The three vows are similarly presented as conditions needed to live the Carmelite ideal. For example, the Carmelites promise obedience to the prior as a representative of Christ and the community. The vow of chastity is understood as a sign of the future to be totally available for God and for one's brothers

---

2 This commentary on the Rule follows Mesters C., O.Carm. "The Carmelite Mystical Tradition in the Service of the Poor" in *Sword*, XLVII, (1987), Nos. 1 & 2, pp. 155-174.

and sisters. It represents a commitment to live human love in its fullness.

The communion of goods expressed by the vow of poverty is a commitment to live as the poor, sharing, begging, and from one's own labor. Through poverty the Carmelites are to be the seed of alternative styles of life in society and the Church.

Chapter two of the rule deals with places to live. This chapter was added by Pope Innocent IV in 1247. It reveals the decision to live in cities as well as rural hermitages. However, not every place was suitable for the Carmelites. It must allow them to live the ideals of the rule, that is, as hermits in community.

The decision on the place of the priory is not left to the prior alone. The prior is to consult with the brethren. This concern about a suitable place to live was a reaction against religious life of the times. The Carmelites were not to forget their roots on Mount Carmel where they were pilgrim-hermits, poor and powerless followers of Christ.

In addition these first six chapters of the rule pay attention to the hermits' cells in relation to that of the prior. The insistence that the prior's cell be located at the entrance of the Wadi was to guarantee that new members and visitors be received by the prior, and not by individual hermits. The prior represents the community. He also represents the norms of the community which guide it in its selection of new members.

3. Chapters 7 to 11: The ideals expressed in the introduction to the rule were modelled on the first community of Christians in Jerusalem. Compare, for example, what the rule proposes with the Acts of the Apostles.

The Rule	Acts
prayer and vigilance	perseverance in prayer
liturgical prayer	frequented the Temple
communion of goods	held everything in common
celebrate of the eucharist	breaking of bread
weekly revision	were one heart and soul

These five points of continuity with the apostolic tradition point to the ways Carmelite community should be lived.

Community must be nourished on the word of God, which demands a commitment to reading Scripture. The technical term for this is "lectio divina" which means not only reading the sacred texts, but having an attitude of openness to the Word of God. This prayerful discernment should be expressed before God, hence the communal celebration of word and sacrament. Community requires simple living so goods could be shared with the poor. The community should be nourished on the Eucharist, and it should be consolidated by weekly revision and coresponsibility by all and for all of its members.

The rule states that the Carmelite is to pray in the cell. Material solitude (the actual cell) is worth nothing without an inner solitude. The cell is a symbol of interiority to which the mind should return when distracted. Solitude is necessary to find oneself and to communicate with others, so as to remain an authentic person and open to people.

The admonition in the rule to meditate and keep vigil on the law of the Lord is a call to focus on the Gospel. This is to take place night and day, that is, whether in or out of the cell. The rule is rooted in Scripture, and Carmelite prayer is deeply biblical. This prayer begins with the cry of the poor, the yearnings of men and women, and through faith leads one on the journey, or pilgrimage, up the mountain of Carmel. It travels the way of the people themselves and assumes a commitment to a journey that is very long and hard, and has no return.

Chapter nine, on the sharing of goods, gave the early hermit an ideal of fraternal living. The sharing of goods is not understood as an end in itself, but rather as a means of conversion to Christ, the poor one, and, as a way to bring the brothers on the side of the poor and into the forefront of a Church being renewed. Through this effort the Carmelites no longer served the feudal lord, but instead served Jesus and Mary. They were to live close to the poor and the powerless, and make the Gospel real for them. This form of life was an alternative for both Church and society.

The rule calls on Carmelites to share daily Eucharist. The chapel is to be in the middle of the cells, which evokes the imagery of Jerusalem. It also evokes the apostles gathered in prayer and Mary in the midst of them.

For the Carmelites on Mount Carmel their chapel was named after St. Mary. They were to celebrate the daily Eucharist in this chapel and in so doing recall the death and resurrection of Jesus.

4. *Chapters 12 to 18:* These chapters deal with the means for carrying out the ideals of the rule. It is in these chapters that Albert made the most extensive use of Scripture. For example, chapter 12 treats fasting. The purpose of fasting was to imitate Jesus, who fasted 40 days in the desert. Fasting was also seen as a means of achieving conversion. However, it also aligned the Carmelite with the poorest people in society who often went hungry. The abstinence from eating meat helped the Carmelite identify with the poor, who almost never had meat.

If chapters 7 to 11 are seen as the heart of the rule, then chapters 14 to 16 are its lifeblood. It presents Carmelite life as a struggle without rest, which must fight against all that dehumanizes men and women, and insert the love of Jesus where there is alienation and hopelessness.

The rule of St. Albert was given to the hermits on Mount Carmel about 1206-1214.

In 1215 the Lateran Council decreed that no new religious orders would be permitted in the Church. This created a problem for the Carmelites, whose approbation had come only from Albert, the Patriarch of Jerusalem. In 1226 Pope Honorius III affirmed that the Carmelites had received their rule before the decree of the Lateran Council and were exempt from its prohibition.

The Muslim advance and constant unrest in the Holy Land encouraged the Carmelites to leave Palestine for Europe. This coming to the west was the occasion for an identity crisis among the Carmelites. They, with sympathetic help from Church leaders, understood their place in the Church of Europe was in the new mendicant movement. They saw themselves as mendicants like the Franciscans, Dominicans, and Augustinians. However, the Carmelites struggled to maintain their eremetical origins during this period of adaptation.

The efforts to adapt Carmelite past in Palestine to the new circumstances in Europe were successful. In 1246 the Carmelites called their first General Chapter, and as a consequence, in 1247, Pope Innocent IV adapted the rule of St. Albert to help the Carmelites live as a mendicant order in Europe.

Mendicants

For St. Francis, the charismatic exponent of medieval mendicancy, poverty was the condition of those who wanted to follow Christ more fully. Francis wanted his friars to preach Christ, by living simply, working for their food, wearing simple habits, like a pilgrim, apostle and disciple. The Carmelite recognized their own unique lifestyle on Mount Carmel was similar to that of the Franciscan in Europe. However, they knew that they were hermit-pilgrims, who could be somewhat like the Franciscans, but not exactly like them.

The first Carmelite constitutions which have been discovered (1281) mentioned that imitation of the mendicants:

> Let the brothers not accept money unless they have permission or unless necessity requires. . . . Likewise, the brothers

shall not presume to travel on horseback. We recommend
that our brothers solicit alms in the most modest way they can
. . . conforming themselves to the method and style of the
Franciscans and Dominicans.[3]

These oldest constitutions of Carmel showed that their
mendicant status was taken for granted. Considering the legislation of the 13th century, the European modifications to the rule
of St. Albert were sufficient to adapt a group of hermits to an
order of friars founded on poverty, dedicated to a prayerful
following of Jesus and to a ministry to the poor. Bound as they
were to a convent, they were religious, travelling apostolically,
and truly mendicants.

Images — Hermit, Pilgrim, Mendicant

These images become vehicles for entering more deeply
into the hearts and minds of the first Carmelites. And because
images express collective depths, they help us come closer to the
souls of the original brothers on Mount Carmel. For Carmelites
this exploration will help to look into the depths of our collective
consciousness, for non-Carmelites it will help them begin a
journey into the center of a spirituality which has enriched the
Church for centuries.

As we have seen, the word hermit calls to mind a prayerful
seeking of Christ in listening and solitude. It means being alone
with Christ, and listening to the whispers of one's own heart. It
means prayerful vigils, it means fasting, it means living on the
fringe. The hermits were those who usually chose not the
ordered life of monasteries, cathedral chapters, or regular

---

3 Cicconetti, C., O.Carm. *The Rule of Carmel* (An Abridgement), The Carmelite Spiritual
  Center, Dareen, IL, 1984, pp. 195-196.

canonries. They sought out the desert — both as a solitary place, or, like St. Anthony and St. Paul, literally the desert of Egypt.

The word pilgrim calls to mind one who seeks Christ by travelling to a holy place. It means the disciple of Christ who wants to go to the ultimate holy place, the Holy Land. Consequently, pilgrims were without family, friends or familiar surroundings. They were powerless and on the margins of society. They travelled simply, with little baggage, and never put down roots, but kept on the move. They sought Christ by serving the alienated, the marginated, the sick and the poor whom they met on their way.

Mendicants conjure up in our mind the poor beggar of Christ. They follow Christ by aligning themselves with the poorest of the poor. They live in simple dwellings and wear the simple clothes of ordinary people, but with distinctive looking habits. They serve Christ by living with and ministering to those who are hungry, sick and have no one to care for them.

Spring — Mountain

Other images used by the early brothers were spring and mountain. They were known as the hermits who lived on Mount Carmel near the Spring of Elijah. The word spring calls to mind water, freshness, life and renewal. The spring is also the sources of water for gardens, and fields — the source of life and refreshment.

The word spring is also a Christological symbol — a fountain of living water; "Come all you who are thirsty. . . ." As well as this, spring is an eschatological symbol indicated by the water flowing from the throne of the Lamb (Rev 21:5; 22:1 etc.). Therefore the spring symbolism suggests that the community's life is drawn from Christ in anticipation of the heavenly Jerusalem.

Mountain means the challenge of a climb and for pilgrims, a tough journey to their goal, the summit. The climber of the mountain has to carry very little, and needs to take periodic rests.

The mountain is both rooted on earth, is solid, substantial, eternal, unchanging, but, also, it reaches to the sky, is mysterious, elusive, hidden — the balance of the incarnational and the eschatological. Carmelites are called to be contemplatives, absorbed in God alone, but as well to serve the people. The ascent of Mount Carmel is a call to face the challenge of prophecy and contemplation. But for Carmelites the spring of Elijah is on Mount Carmel which implies their following Christ demands keeping their feet on the ground, while at the same time, reaching for the elusive heights of the peak, often hidden from view.

Implications for our lives

We have seen that the first Carmelites were hermit-pilgrim -mendicants. Their source and roots were on the holy mountain of Carmel. They were a group of people who wanted to come closer to Christ, by being poor and powerless, who wanted to serve Christ in the alienated and oppressed. They searched the Scriptures and in ministry and preaching passed on the word of hope to those who had no one to care for them. The rule of St. Albert called them to a very simple lifestyle, as a solitary traveller seeking the naked Christ.

Whether we are Carmelites or not we can learn from the first brothers of Mount Carmel. We need to learn the value of solitude and silence in a prayerful seeking, to come close to Jesus. We need to learn of the liberating experiences of the pilgrims of Christ, who seek their Lord separated from the everyday power structures of Church and society. There are risks to be taken in leaving familiar territory in order to find Christ. It is fearful to leave family and friends, where we are known and respected. But the pilgrim seeker is prepared to give up everything to find Christ. How much are we prepared to give up in order to come close to him?

The spirit of the mendicants is the spirit of simple beggars for Christ, who not only beg for themselves, but for those who have no voice. The mendicants propose an alternative lifestyle which puts the prayerful seeking of Christ at the heart of their communal living. We need to learn the value of simple living and giving one's life for the service of the poor. They teach us that what we earn is not really ours, but is given to us by God to share with those who have very little. They teach us to speak out, when injustice grinds people into hopelessness. They use any resources they have for those who have nothing.

The spirit of Carmel calls the Church and society to a continual seeking of Christ. It also challenges us to stand beside the alienated and powerless. It calls us to do these things in solitary prayer, in climbing like a pilgrim, toward the holy mountain, which is Christ, and in serving and ministering to the poor.

Appendix: The rule of St. Albert given between 1206-1214

Note: *For the purpose of comparison, changes in St. Albert's original rule made by Pope Innocent IV are indicated by brackets i.e. (Inn.) Where this occurred Albert's original is indicated by brackets (Alb.). The translation is by Bede Edwards, OCD, in* The Rule of St. Albert, *1973.*

Introduction: St. Albert, called by God's favor to be Patriarch of the church of Jerusalem, bids health in the Lord and the blessing of the

Holy Spirit to his beloved sons in Christ, B. and the other hermits under obedience to him, who live near the spring on Mount Carmel.

Many and varied are the ways in which our saintly forefathers laid down how everyone, whatever his station or the kind of religious observance he has chosen, should live a life of allegiance to Jesus Christ — how, pure in heart and stout in conscience, he must be unswerving in the service of his Master. It is to me, however, that you have come for a rule of life in keeping with your avowed purpose, a rule you may hold fast to henceforward; and therefore:

Chapter 1: The first thing I require is for you to have a prior, one of yourselves, who is to be chosen for the office by common consent, or that of the greater or maturer part of you. Each of the others must promise him obedience — of which, once promised, he must try to make his deeds the true reflection — (Inn.) and also chastity and the renunciation of ownership.

Chapter 2: (Inn.) If the prior and the brothers see fit, you may have foundations in solitary places, or where you are given a site that is suitable and convenient for the observance proper to your Order.

Chapter 3: Next, each one of you is to have a separate cell, situated as the lie of the land you propose to occupy may dictate, and allotted by disposition of the prior with agreement of the other brothers, or the more mature among them.

Chapter 4: (Inn.) However, you are to eat whatever may have been given you in a common refectory, listening together meanwhile to a reading from Holy Scripture where that can be done without difficulty.

Chapter 5: None of the brothers is to occupy a cell other than that allotted to him or to exchange cells with another, without leave of whoever is prior at the time.

Chapter 6: The prior's cell should stand near the entrance to your property, so that he may be the first to meet those who approach, and whatever has to be done in consequence may all be carried out as he may decide and order.

Chapter 7: Each one of you is to stay in his cell or nearby, pondering the Lord's law day and night and keeping watch at his prayers unless attending to some other duty.

Chapter 8: (Alb.) Those who know their letters, and how to read the psalms, should, for each of the hours, say those our holy forefathers laid down and the approved custom of the Church appoints for that hour. Those who do not know their letters must say 25 Our Fathers for the night office, except on Sundays and solemnities when that number is to be doubled so that the Our Father is said 50 times; the same prayer must be said seven times in the morning in the place of Lauds, and seven times too for each of the other hours, except for Vespers when it must be said 15 times.

(Inn.) Those who know how to say the canonical hours with those in Orders should do so, in the way those holy forefathers of ours laid down, and according to the Church's approved custom. Those who do not know the hours must say 25 Our Fathers for the night office, except on Sundays and solemnities when that number is to be doubled so that the our Father is said 50 times; the same prayer must be said seven times in the morning place of Lauds, and seven times too for each of the other hours, except for Vespers when it must be said 15 times.

Chapter 9: (Alb.) None of the brothers must lay claim to anything as his own, but your property is to be held in common; and of such things as the Lord may have given you each is to receive from the prior — that is the man he appoints for the purpose — whatever befits his age and needs. However, as I have said, each one of you is to stay in his own allotted cell, and live, by himself, on what is given out to him.

(Inn.) None of the brothers is to lay claim to anything as his own, but you are to possess everything in common; and each is to receive from the prior — that is the brother he appoints for the purpose — whatever befits his age and needs. (Inn.) You may have as many asses and mules as you need, however, and may keep a certain amount of livestock or poultry.

Chapter 10: An oratory should be built as conveniently as possible among the cells, where, if it can be done without difficulty, you are to gather each morning to hear Mass.

Chapter 11: On Sundays too, or other days if necessary, you should discuss matters of discipline and your spiritual welfare; and on this occasion indiscretions and failings of the brothers, if any be found at fault, should be lovingly corrected.

Chapter 12: You are to fast every day, except Sundays, from the feast of the Exaltation of the Holy Cross until Easter Day, unless bodily sickness or feebleness, or some other good reason, demand a dispensation from the fast; for necessity overrides every law.

Chapter 13: (Alb.) You are always to abstain from meat, unless it has to be eaten as a remedy for sickness or great feebleness.

(Inn.) You are to abstain from meat, except as a remedy for sickness or feebleness. But as, when you are on a journey, you more often than not have to beg your way; outside your own houses you may eat foodstuffs that have been cooked with meat, so as to avoid giving trouble to your hosts. At sea, however, meat may be eaten.

Chapter 14: Since man's life on earth is a time of trial, and all who live devotedly in Christ must undergo persecution, and the devil your foe is on the prowl like a roaring lion looking for prey to devour, you must use every care to clothe yourselves in God's armor so that you may be ready to withstand the enemy's ambush. Your loins are to be girt with chastity, your breast fortified by holy meditations, for, as Scripture has it, holy meditation will save you. Put on holiness as your breastplate, and it will enable you to love the Lord your God with all your heart and soul and strength, and your neighbor as yourself. Faith must be your shield on all occasions, and with it you will be able to quench all the flaming missiles of the wicked one; there can be no pleasing God without faith; (and the victory lies in your faith). On your head set the helmet of salvation, and so be sure of deliverance by our only Savior, who sets his own free from their sins. The sword of the spirit, the word of God, must abound in your mouths and hearts. Let all you do have the Lord's word for accompaniment.

Chapter 15: You must give yourselves to work of some kind, so that the devil may always find you busy; no idleness on your part must give him a chance to pierce the defenses of your souls. In this respect you have both the teaching and the example of St. Paul the Apostle, into whose mouth Christ put his own words. God made him preacher and teacher of faith and truth to the nations: with him as your leader you cannot go astray. We live among you, he said, laboring and weary, toiling night and day so as not to be a burden to any of you; not because we have no power to do otherwise but so as to give you, in your own selves, an example you might imitate. For the charge we gave you when we were with you was this: that whoever is not willing to work should not be allowed to eat either. For we have heard that there are certain restless idlers among you. We charge people of this kind, and implore them in the name of our Lord Jesus Christ, that they earn their own bread by silent toil. This is the way of holiness and goodness: see that you follow it.

Chapter 16: The Apostle would have us keep silence, for in silence he tells us to work. As the prophet also makes known to us: Silence is the way to foster holiness. Elsewhere he says: Your strength will lie in silence and hope. (Alb.) For this reason I lay down that you are to keep silence from Vespers until Terce the next day, unless some necessary or some good reason, or the prior's permission, should break the silence. (Inn.) For this reason I lay down that you are to keep silence from after Compline until after Prime the next day. At other times, although you need not keep silence so strictly, be careful not to indulge in a great deal of talk, for, as Scripture has it — and experience teaches us no less — sin will not be wanting where there is much talk, and he who is careless in speech will come to harm; and elsewhere: The use of many words brings harm to the speaker's soul. And Our Lord says in the Gospel: Every rash word uttered will have to be accounted for on Judgment Day. Make a balance then, each of you, to weigh his words in; keep a tight rein on your mouths, lest you should stumble and fall in speech, and your fall be irreparable and prove mortal. Like the Prophet, watch your step lest your tongue give offense, and employ every care in keeping silent, which is the way to foster holiness.

Chapter 17: You, brother B., and whoever may succeed you as prior, must always keep in mind and put into practice what our Lord said in the Gospel: Whoever has a mind to become a leader among you must make himself servant to the rest, and whichever of you would be first must become your bondsman.

Chapter 18: You other brothers too, hold your prior in humble reverence, your minds not on him but on Christ who has placed him over you, and who, to those who rule the churches, addressed the words: Whoever pays you heed pays heed to me, and whoever treats you with dishonor dishonors me; if you remain so minded you will not be found guilty of contempt, but will merit life eternal as fit reward for your obedience.

Here then are a few points I have written down to provide you with a standard of conduct to live up to; but our Lord, at his Second Coming will reward anyone who does more than he is obliged to do. See that the bond of common sense is the guide of the virtues.

For reflection: individuals or groups

1. How much of the hermit is in your spiritual life? Is the image "hermit" applicable to you? Would you like more of the "hermit" to be part of your life? Why? What will you do to achieve this?

2. How much does the image "pilgrim" apply to your spiritual experience? Does it bring suffering into your life? How do you cope with the negative and positive side of the pilgrim in you?

Hints for writing and sharing:

See the end of the introduction

References used in Chapter 1

Cicconetti, C., O.Carm., *The Rule of Carmel*, (An Abridgement) The Carmelite Spiritual Center, Darien, IL, 1984.

Clarke, H., O.Carm. and Edwards, B., OCD (Eds.), *The Rule of Saint Albert*, Vinea Carmeli, Aylesford, 1973.

Leyser, H., *Hermits and the New Monasticism*. Macmillan, London, 1984.

Mesters, C., O.Carm., "The Carmelite Mystical Tradition at the Service of the Poor," in Blanchard, D., O.Carm. (Ed.) *Liberation Spirituality: Carmelite Perspectives*. Sword 47 (1987) pp. 155-174.

Secondin, B., O.Carm., "Carmelite Fraternity and Christian Community: the Rule of Carmel between Past and Present," in *Nubecula* 36 2 & 3 (1985), pp. 1-44.

Elijah

Carmelites see themselves as sons and daughters of the prophet, Elijah. Because they were hermit-pilgrims living a life of silence and prayer on Mount Carmel, they felt a close association with Elijah. They did not just pluck this association out of the air. The desert fathers always saw John the Baptist and Elijah as models for hermits and monks. However, Mount Carmel was a holy place because Elijah, the Tishbite, had done great things for God there. It is not surprising then that the Latin hermits who settled on Mount Carmel took Elijah as a model to imitate. Jacques de Vitry, the Bishop of Acre from 1216-1228, described, "the hermits on Mount Carmel as leading solitary lives in imitation of the holy anchorite, Elijah, where like bees of the Lord, they laid up sweet spiritual honey in little comb-like cells."

The Fathers of the Church saw religious life as a response to a Gospel call. Since they reasoned that the New Testament is foreshadowed in the Old Testament, therefore, there should be types of the monastic life in the Old Testament. Thus, the Fathers saw Elijah as such a type. Some of the early Fathers, for example Justin and Irenaeus, offer Elijah as the model for the perfect life. Origen cites Elijah as a proof of the efficacy of prayer, while Athanasius, in his Life of Anthony, recalls the saying of the Father of religious life that all who make profession

of the solitary life must take the great Elijah as their model and
see in his life what their lives must be. The monastic movement
of the fourth century took Elijah as the model for the monk,
emphasizing his celibacy, his poverty, his dwelling in the desert,
his prayer and fasting. Jerome refers to the tradition which sees
the prophet Elijah as the first monk to inhabit the desert.

It was on this patristic basis that the early Carmelite
authors based the order's connection with Elijah. This, and the
fact that they settled on the holy Mount Carmel, brought them
into contact with the Old and New Testament traditions concerning Elijah.

Today's Carmelites would want to stress Eliajh's role as a
champion of the people, and the embodiment of the faith of the
community of the anawim (the remnant of the People of God).

When the Carmelites took Elijah as a patron of their
Order, they followed the spirituality of the time and saw him as a
model of the eremitical life. Throughout the history of the
Order, Carmelite authors have seen Elijah as model of prayerful
contemplation and prophetic action. This chapter will take a
brief look at the biblical evidence and will show how this
interpretation came into the Carmelite tradition; then Elijah as a
figure who protects the poor and the alienated; how Carmelites
are called to take an option for the poor; and, finally, how Elijah
is an archetype for all believers in general and Carmelites in
particular.

Elijah in the Bible [1]

The Elijah saga-cycle is to be found in that part of Scripture
starting from his sudden appearance in 1 Kings 17:1 and ending

1 This section (pp. 24-27) owes a debt of gratitude to the research of Chalmers, J., O.Carm., "The
   Prophetic model of Religious Life: The Role of the Prophet Elijah in Carmelite Spirituality," in
   Nubecula 36 (1985), No. 1.

with his being taken up to heaven in the fiery chariot in 2 Kings 2:13. The background of the Book of Kings is the effort to show how the monarchy was a failure. The context of the Elijah stories is the struggle between the true religion and pagan influences. Yahweh was the God of the Israelites, who had brought them out of Egypt and given them a Promised Land. The God of the Hebrews was not one to look for elbow room on an Olympus with a lot of other gods. "You shall have no Gods except me" (Dt 5:7). At the time of Elijah, the pagan customs of the neighboring Canaanites had become strongly embedded among the common people in Israel. There was a strong possibility that adherence to the God of the Exodus would be wiped out.

Elijah appeared on the scene at a very critical moment in this struggle. Ahab, the King of Israel, married Jezebel, princess of Tyre. Her religion was called Baalism, which was based on the idea that humans must relate to and appease the mysterious powers that surround and support them. This was done through ritual, and these powers were often personified and made into gods — Baalism. Jezebel was allowed, together with her servants, to continue to practice her religion in Israel. A temple of Baal was built for her in Samaria (1 K 6:32. f.). However, Jezebel maintained 450 prophets of Baal, and 400 prophets of Asherah. Jezebel and her court actively campaigned to convert the Israelites to her religion. She was determined to wipe out faith in the God of the Israelites, and to substitute Baal for Yahweh. Jezebel remained in the memory of the people of Israel as the one who had invited the King to sin against Yahweh.

Ahab's acceptance of his wife's religion and culture had political overtones. He saw this as a means to unify the Israelites and Canaanites. In doing so he was carrying on the policy of his father, King Omri. The marriage of Ahab and Jezebel was a move in the attempt to unify the kingdom. However, the prophet Elijah was the leader of the opposition to this betrayal of Yahweh.

The scriptural stories of Elijah show a prophet who was actively involved in the problems of his times as the mouthpiece of Yahweh, upholding the true religion of Israel. The main reason for the Elijah cycle being included in the Deuteronomic history was that Elijah was the instrument used by God to preserve the true religion in Israel — a truly critical moment in the history of God's people.

Elijah, as God's prophet, was both contemplative and active in his response to God's call. He was a person who was totally at God's disposal. He stood before Yahweh like a servant waiting instruction (1 K 7:1; 18:15, 36). This implied Elijah was in a constant state of prayer. He, like all the prophets, was dominated by the Word of God. The subject of the Elijah saga was not the prophet himself but Yahweh, whose Word was not simply something to reflect on in solitude and silence, but a fire to burn evil out of the hearts of people. Total openness to God's word led Elijah to live a very special style of life.

He was a visible sign of Israel; a sign which challenged the whole people. He did not live like others but stood out as a criticism of their lives and values. The prophet could be a sign to others only because first of all he himself had been grasped by the Word of God. Elijah was a person of mystery. He was famous for his sudden appearances and disppearances (cf. 1 K 8:12). His final disappearance in the fiery chariot left a lasting impression on God's people.

Two characteristics of Elijah stand out — his faithfulness and his creativity. He was faithful to the true religious tradition of Israel, being the champion of covenant fidelity in a day when the covenant nearly disappeared. He refused to allow anyone to take away his religion. God alone was the Lord of Israel and Elijah would take no interference in Yahweh's domain by the Baals of Jezebel.

On the other hand, Elijah was not afraid to be creative in religious matters. As the people settled in Israel, they began to forget the God who had seemed to fit in well with their experiences in the desert, but did not seem to have much to say to their new life in the Promised Land. The Israelites tended to adopt the worship of Baal who was more useful to farmers as he was supposed to be master of the rain and the sunshine and lord of fertility. The image of their God Yahweh was in serious need of "modernization." If he was the true God of every situation in which Israel might find herself, it was Elijah who succeeded in transforming the image of Yahweh who commanded the rain, who sent fire from heaven, it was Yahweh who was the one and only God of Israel and not Baal.

Elijah and Carmelite Spirituality

So far we have seen Elijah as he was in the biblical tradition, now we shall see what effect he has on Carmelite spirituality. The order sees Elijah as patron and spiritual father. The characteristics of the prophet — fidelity to tradition and creativity are basic to understanding Carmel in the past and present.

Joseph Chalmers says that every Christian is called to be perfect (Mt 5:48). However, this perfection cannot be reached in a day; it requires constant growth. The Christian life is a continuous becoming with many stages striving towards maturity in Christ. In the Hebrew Scriptures we see how Yahweh taught Israel with great patience and over a long period of time. In the Christian Scriptures we see a gradual deepening of faith. The Christian cannot stand still; but must strive for a fullness of life in Christ. Jesus, himself, was not immune from this basic Christian experience — "and Jesus increased in wisdom, in stature, and in favor with God and people" (Lk 2:52).

The Carmelite order has followed and is following this law

of growth, throughout its history. This must be the path of any order which takes the prophet, Elijah, as its spiritual father. The word of the prophets was always directed to their own situation. They were always modern because they sought new answers to new problems. Prophets always opposed the idea that history has been fulfilled, and that there are no new challenges. So Carmelites, following the spirit of Elijah, must not only be faithful to the traditions of the past, but must be creative when faced with new challenges.

Elijah was a man of vision. He used his experience of God in silence and solitude to clothe the word of God in a garb suitable for his times. So too, Carmelites listen to the word of God in a garb suitable for their times. They hear God in prayer, experience the signs of the times in reflective contemplation, and face the challenges of their own times. This is how they live according to the inspiration of the prophet, Elijah.

As Elijah was a person deeply committed to the religious traditions of his people, so too, Carmelites must be faithful to their tradition of prayer in silence and solitude, contemplation and mysticism. The order has produced men and women who have attained mystical experience of God, perhaps with a concept of the world not in tune with today's outlook. Elijah did not simply repeat the past, but wanted to reinterpret the tradition in the light of new circumstances. Faithfulness among Carmelites is not clinging to the past, but rethinking the tradition of the Order in creative ways. The spirituality of Carmel must continually ask how being intimate with God and listening to his word can be done in the world of today.

The Order forms part of the mendicant tradition, which not only lived in simplicity and poverty, but served the Church with an active apostolate. With Elijah there was no conflict between prayer and activity. So Carmelites, like Elijah, can be both faithful to the traditions of the Order, and yet creative in applying this tradition to modern problems. When Carmelites are creative, they are open to growth. Therefore, by following the prophet Elijah, Carmelites are called to be prophets in the Church. For the prophet there is a combination of contemplation on the word and active service of the Church and the world. A Carmelite is one who seeks the face of God; a Carmelite is one who hears God's word both in the tradition and in the world about him/her. Consequently, modern Carmelites see their prophetic lives to be lived as a fundamental option for the poor. To read Carmelite tradition from the perspective of the poor is to imitate our forefathers. It is a case of fidelity.

Elijah and the Poor

In Elijah's time the people had forgotten their tradition of caring for the poor, the widows, the orphans, and those who were oppressed. The original enthusiasm which in times past had given Israel strength and originality had been forgotten. The king, Ahab, had changed the tradition. This reinterpretation suited Ahab and Jezebel to strengthen their kingdom and forget God's commands. Ahab's turning away from the God of Israel would take no opposition. When he challenged this betrayal of Yahweh, Elijah was considered a traitor to the King and the nation.

Ahab's betrayal of God had economic, social and political consequences for the people of God. Ahab became master of commerce, took money and goods from the poor, built his marble palace and temple of Baal in Samaria. He robbed the poor and murdered when necessary to gain his ends. When the country was stricken by drought his only concern was for his horses (army) and donkeys (commerce). That means his only concern was power and money, not the stricken people of God. The King tried to hide the face of Yahweh from the people and stifle the cry of the poor.

Carlos Mesters[2] notes that to understand Elijah's opposition and intervention we need to look at the three functions of the Elijah tradition: first the tradition; second the situation of the oppressed; third Elijah himself.

First, Elijah relived the Exodus journey of the people. He went to Karith and relived spiritually the experience of God's people when Moses led them out of captivity in Egypt. He experienced denunciation, and the hunger and thirst of the desert. He became one with God's people by remaking their Exodus.

Second, Elijah sought out the favorites of God among his people — the poor. This is evident in his going to the widow of Sarephtha. She was a widow, and a stranger. All these characteristics described the alienated people, those whom King Ahab did not want in his kingdom. In contrast to Ahab, the widow preserved the ideal of sharing, with the capacity to recognize God's call to life. In other words, she preserved the ideal of the covenant. Elijah prayed at the request of the widow and his prayer became an expression of the cry of the poor. In the end the widow gave her witness: "You are a man of God."

In his search for the true God of Israel Elijah went to the tradition and to the poor. However, the search for God does not end in the tradition or in the people. God surpasses both, as was indicated by Elijah's journey to Mount Horeb where he learned that God was not in the storm, the earthquake, the lightning — all signs that accompanied the giving of the law to Moses. Instead Elijah found God in the gentle breeze. In his journey to God Elijah passed through the tradition, contacted the poor, and walked in darkness and reflection to find Yahweh, the living God. Elijah, as we will see later in the chapter, stands out as an archetype, an everyman figure, by his scriptural experience and

2 Mesters, C., O.Carm., "The Carmelite Mystical Tradition at the Service of the Poor," in D. Blanchard, O.Carm. (Ed.) *Liberation Spirituality: Carmelite Perspectives*, Sword 67 (1987).

his journeys. People often find it easy to identify with many biblical personalities, because of the universal nature of their experiences — Elijah is such a one.

Mester believes that by passing through these three functions — the reliving of the Exodus experience, seeking the favorites of God, and seeking the true God of Israel — Elijah gradually distanced himself from Ahab and Jezebel and their re-interpretation of the tradition of Israel's history. Elijah became the leader of the opposition to Baal and his prophets. As a prophet of God he stood for Yahweh against the prevailing religious, social and political structures, and with the poor and the alienated. He was a faithful prophet, and God blessed the people through him and his ministry. Elijah was creative in re-establishing worship of Yahweh. In the end, Yahweh defended Elijah and once again freed the people.

Carmelites and the Poor

Carmelites share a vocation to seek the face of God. The face of God is revealed in the poor in two ways. The poor are an expression of God's denunciation of injustice. Our Carmelite tradition tells us to seek the presence of God in the gentle breeze. This is the God who unseats the powerful and raises up the humble. Before Carmelites can be practitioners of mysticism, we must learn to be disciples and apprentices. This demands a conversion of life and an identity with the poor and alienated. This is a prophetic message which Carmelites have for today's Church and society.

Carmelites need to analyze critically what our mystical tradition has to offer the poor of today's world. Often poor people live contemplation; they climb Mount Carmel and pass through the dark night, but rarely understand what our spiritual theologians and writers are saying. This is often because

Carmelites may be speaking to an elite few. Carmelites often deal with individual problems and do not pay sufficient attention to unjust structures. These structures alienate people and keep them oppressed. Carmelites may be in danger of not being faithful to the traditions of Elijah and Jesus who walked among the people, and struggled against infidelity to God's word. The lives of today's poor can provide Carmelites with a better understanding of our tradition.

The Elijah tradition calls Carmelites to prophecy. The prophetic dimension of Carmelite spirituality challenges men and women of Carmel to be immersed in the world of their own times. They, like the prophets of old, need to have an attitude of openness to the word of God, to be attentive to the signs of the times, and need to speak out against injustices wherever they see them. They need to seek the face of God both in solitude, like Elijah but also in the alienated, like Elijah did in the heart of the widow. As the prophets were the heart and conscience of Israel, so Carmelites need to be the same for the Church and stress Elijah's role as a champion of the people and the embodiment of the faith of the community. The prophetic model for Carmelite life helps to give a deeper understanding of vowed life.

Chastity

Consecrated chastity is a demonstration to the world of the possibility of love. Our times seem to be involved in a never ending search for the kind of pleasure which depersonalizes many fellow humans. Consecrated chastity in religious life is a positive commitment to others, and those who live this vow want to mirror the concern God has for all people. Religious are so in love with God and all his creation that they are incapable of giving themselves in love exclusively to one person. They make themselves eunuchs for the sake of the Kingdom (Mt 19:12).

This is a witness to the absolute transcendence of God and to the universality of Christian love, because religious pledge themselves to all those whom God sends them. This involvement of the whole of one's life as a sign to others is prophetic witness. From that moment on the prophet and the religious are totally involved in God.

The function of this prophetic form of love in the Church and in the world is to make religious different within the context of the universal call to holiness. It calls all Christians back to the authentic, faithful, loving and joyful gift of self which is the mark of all Christians, whether they be celibate or married. In the Carmelite tradition there is a link between contemplation and chastity — having a heart free for concentration on the love of God, and openness to the mystery of every person.

Poverty

The voluntary poverty and simple lifestyle of religious is prophetic because it condemns the oppression of the poor, and the idolatry of wealth, which are evils in our world. The prophets of the Bible criticized these vices. One of the best examples of condemnation of injustice is when Elijah condemned King Ahab for acquiring Naboth's vineyard by violent means (1 K 21). Modern religious witness to the need for all to share in the good things of God's creation. The religious must prophesy against all that divides person from person, especially oppression, alienation and grinding poverty. These divisions are also found in the Christian Churches and their structures. The religious vowed to poverty and simplicity must live the Gospel as a sort of counter-culture to the Church and the world.

The vowed life of poverty, which is a radical sharing of all that we have and all that we are, takes on this prophetic function. Carmelites have publicly committed themselves to showing by their shared life, that true humanity and Christianity can be lived in the Church and fired by the same ideals which fire all vowed religious, Christians and the whole Church.

Obedience

Vowed to obedience, Carmelites are prophetic in the Church and the world by making everyone consider the correct use of power and authority. The prophets of the Bible not only sought the face of God but were totally obedient to his call. They were chosen by God to speak his word to the world; vowed religious follow Jesus who completely followed the will of God. In this, religious witness to the place God should have in the Church and the world.

Francis Moloney[3] says that this is at the heart of Christian calling. All Christians are called to follow Jesus in obedience like the prophets. We must be seen as living under the divine urgency to love in the plan of our mysterious God. In this way we will continue to proclaim to the people among whom we live, the freedom which a radical openness to God creates. We can be a challenge and worry to an over-institutionalized Church, over bureaucratized democracies, and dictatorial totalitarian states. Our freely chosen vow of obedience keeps posing awkward questions to the Church and secular organizations — such as, why are you instituted?

Elijah Archetype

John Welch[4] has shown how Carl Jung, the psychologist, chose Elijah as an example of an archetype because the Elijah

---

3 Moloney, F., SDB, *Disciples and Prophets*, Darton, Longman and Todd, London, 1980, p. 168.
4 Welch, J., O.Carm., *Spiritual Pilgrims*, Paulist Press, NY, 1982, pp. 82-83.

stories contain mythical elements and because posterity has added legends to Elijah. We are dealing with an archetype. For Jung archetypes are primordial images common to all humankind. By primordial images Jung did not mean specific images and ideas, but predispositions or patterns. Archetypes have also been called channels, watercourses and imprints. They are similar to negatives which need to be developed.

Jung found common elements in all peoples and cultures, in their stories, dreams, fairytales, and mythology. These are birth, death, rebirth, resurrection, journey, hero, wise old man, earth-mother and God. These archetypes provide patterns of meaning and guides to developing one's personality. A person's conscious experience is what gives an archetype specific content. Archetypes cannot be known in themselves. They become symbols which help the individual to understand his/her experiences of life.

For Jung Elijah is a powerful archetype which has given birth to new forms of understanding. One of these phenomena was the first Carmelites' choice of Elijah as their spiritual father.

Jung believes that the archetype gets itself chosen rather than being deliberately chosen. He says that the first Carmelites would have felt an almost unconscious and natural attraction to Elijah. This would be because of the very atmosphere of Mount Carmel — a holy place, holy to the Canaanites, Phoenicians, Greeks, Romans and Hebrews. Today it is still holy to Druses, Christians, Jews and, of course, Carmelites. Jung believes that the Carmelite hermits were influenced by the legend of Elijah because Mount Carmel and Elijah are inextricably linked. This is why Elijah is still a powerful archetype to Moslems, Jews and Christians who today make pilgrimages to Mount Carmel, a sacred site linked to the holy prophet, Elijah.

According to Jung when an archetype becomes known to the consciousness, it does so through a symbol. Many things we understand only partially, but a symbol helps us to understand more about ourselves and our world. It transforms energy in our unconscious into an equivalent conscious form. The symbol is not consciously created, but is a spontaneous formation out of the unconscious. This symbol is pregnant with meaning and is generative of new understandings.

So the early Carmelites were led to a deeper understanding of themselves when they reflected on Elijah, the prophet. They were called to a similar prophetic life on Mount Carmel. Although they were physically living on Mount Carmel, both Elijah and the holy mountain became archetype and symbol for their lives. Then they understood that even if they did not physically live on Mount Carmel, they would always be called to climb the holy mountain and live the prophetic form of life in whatever place or whatever time.

For reflection: individuals or groups

1. *Who are the prophets for you in your life? How much do you imitate them? Do you see yourself as a prophet? In what sense?*

2. *Who are the heroes and heroines in your life? How much of "hermit," "pilgrim," "prophet," "mendicant," (or any other image which relates to your heroes and heroines) is in them?*

Hints for writing and sharing:

See the end of the introduction

References used in Chapter 2

Chalmers, J., O.Carm., "The Prophetic Model of Religious Life: The Role of the Prophet Elijah in Carmelite Spirituality," in *Nubecula*, 36 (1985) No. 1.

Mesters, C., O.Carm., "The Carmelite Mystical Tradition at the Service of the Poor," in Blanchard, D., O.Carm. (Ed.) "Liberation Spirituality: Carmelite Perspectives," *Sword* 67 (1987).

Moloney, F., SDB. *Disciples and Prophets*, Darton, Longman and Todd, London, 1980.

Welch, J., O.Carm. *Spiritual Pilgrims*, Paulist Press, New York, 1982.

Mary and Carmel

From the beginning the hermits on Mount Carmel had a special devotion to Mary, the Mother of Jesus. The brothers had a simple chapel at the center of their cells dedicated to St. Mary, the Lady of the Place, or the Lady of the Manor — Our Lady of Mount Carmel. In this chapter we will investigate how Carmelites see Mary as Patroness, Virgin Mother, Sister and Beauty of Carmel.

Patroness of Carmelites

Patronage was an accepted reality of the middle ages. Vassals would express their belonging to a patron in both words and gestures, like placing their hands in his, a custom that still survives at religious professions. Patronage involved two persons, with mutual rights and obligations. The lord of the manor undertook to protect the subject, or vassal, who in turn promised service. The rule of St. Albert stressed that the Carmelite has an allegiance to Jesus Christ, as the feudal vassal had to his lord. The Latin term in the rule, "obsequium Jesu Christi" is usually translated, "in the footsteps of Jesus Christ." This translation tends to miss the original meaning of the mutual bond of responsible lordship and loyal service. The first hermits of

Carmel thought it was natural that they would have a similar allegiance to the mother of Jesus, their Lord. Consequently, in the feudal logic, they had not only a Lord of the Manor, but a Lady of the Manor, or *the Lady of the Place*. When the hermits on Mount Carmel dedicated their oratory to Mary the Lady of the Manor, they regarded themselves as bound, feudal style, to her service, under her protection and patronage. Their religious lives were in her constant care; they were her concern and she was theirs.

The initial understanding of the bond between the Carmelites and Mary continued as a strong tradition thoughout the writing of medieval Carmelites. The sense of special dedication appears early in the extant documents of the Order, for example, in those from the general Chapter of Montpellier 1287. This was the chapter at which the white cloak replaced the earlier, and somewhat Palestinian, striped mantle of the first hermit brothers. As the Carmelites moved into the European mainstream of the mendicants, they began to send students to the universities. This General Chapter said, "we beg the prayers of the glorious Virgin Mary, in whose service and honor our institute of Mount Carmel was founded." The Marian tradition of the medieval Carmelites was summed up by the friar, Arnold Bostius, in a work entitled, "The Patronage of Mary and the Exercise of that Patronage with respect to the Order of Carmel that bears her name." The primitive understanding of the Carmelite dedication to Mary, the Lady of the Manor, was to the Mother of Jesus, with an emphasis on her virginity, her purity, and her motherhood.

Title of the Order

This stress grew stronger in a later controversy, which concerned the very survival of the Order. As late comers to

Europe, the Brothers of St. Mary of Mount Carmel were not welcomed by some. They had to justify their right to exist as a separate Order and be counted among the mendicant friars, as well as face the opposition of some bishops and diocesan clergy. They had to show that they lived on Mount Carmel according to a rule of life given by St. Albert, Patriarch of Jerusalem (d. 1214). They pointed out that they were living a regular life prior to the restrictive legislation of the Fourth Lateran Council in 1215. Even as late as 1274 — the Second Council of Lyons, the issue was still in doubt and was resolved by Pope Boniface VIII.

As early as 1252 the title, the Brothers of Our Lady of Mount Carmel, appears in a letter written to the Order from Pope Innocent IV. The early Carmelites struggled to retain the name of the Order as the Brothers of Our Lady of Mount Carmel because the philosophers and theologians of the middle ages attached enormous value to the name of something as conveying its inner essence. Consequently, the prayer from the Carmelite liturgy of the Mass of the Feast of Our Lady of Mount Carmel, 16 July, reveals this struggle.

> Lord God,
> You willed that the Order of Carmel should be named in
> honor of the Blessed Virgin Mary,
> Mother of your Son.
> Through her prayers as we honor her today bring us to
> your holy Mountain,
> Christ our Lord,
> who lives and reigns . . .

Virgin and Mother

The medieval Carmelites found in Mary's virginity a model for their own lives. Even the legends they loved emphasized virginity. They loved to say that they were linked to virginal prophets Elijah and Elisha, because of the presence of holy hermits living on Mount Carmel right back to the time of Elijah. They emphasized the fact that Elijah was the first man to practice voluntary virginity, and Mary the first woman to do so. In their life of dedicated chastity they were therefore, living in the imitation of both. Because of the virginity they had in common with her, they thought of Mary as their sister.

Brothers in the title of the Order had the meaning of a group of brothers, like other religious, brothers to one another and to the poor people they served as begging friars. However, the Carmelites developed this idea into a special sense of brotherhood, with Mary as sister, whom they were to imitate with their own virginal lives.

If they imitate Mary they realized they would find her constant and faithful. This would resonate with such titles as Virgin most pure, in defense of the Immaculate Conception, which was the Order's patronal feast before 16 July. The white cloak worn by the Carmelites was seen as a symbol of Mary's purity.

They understood purity as not simply the absence of sin, nor even simply chastity but the offering of oneself totally to God, as Mary did, nothing held back, giving God a pure heart. The picture of Mary as the most pure Virgin reflects the ideal of the Order as found in one of the earliest writings, the Book of the Institution of the First Monks: "to offer to God a heart holy and pure from all stain of sin."

The most pure virginity of Mary has for us today important contemporary relevance. It can lead us to examine the riches of virginity in its narrower sense of celibacy to show it as giving a possibility of a full flowering of the whole person, in spirit as well as body, in a rich and fulfilled life in service of the Church and society. However, the most pure virginity of Mary is more than that. It is her complete availability before God; "I am the handmaid of the Lord," (Lk 1:38). She is above all the one "who heard the word of God and kept it" (Lk 11:28). She was praised for her faith, as she pondered God's will in her heart. Her most pure heart, desiring only that God's will be done, shows us the way to renewed Christian and Carmelite authenticity.

Medieval patronage developed gradually into the concept of consecration. Consecration in the first place is an act of religion, and as such can be made only to God. Hence, to speak of consecration to Our Lady is an adapted use of the word for a particular form of devotion to Mary, and one of special intensity.

In Christian and Carmelite life, begun in baptism, renewed through religious vows, what comes first is always the grace of God. Carmelite consecration has two focal points.

The first is a consecration to God in the spirit of Mary. The second is God consecrates us through giving us Mary, Our Lady of Mount Carmel, as our patroness, sister and mother — we are consecrated by receiving this great gift. The gift must mean what was meant for the beloved disciple at the foot of the cross on Calvary. We Carmelites take Mary into our own, both the person of Mary and the community of which she is the embodiment, that is the Church, the body of Christ, and more specifically the Carmelite family. Carmelite spirituality implies a dedication to the acceptance of the gift of Mary from Jesus, and a deeper commitment to the Church.

Spiritual Mother

Mary as the spiritual mother of Carmelites is a central theme in the spiritual tradition. We are her sons and daughters, as indeed are all the brothers and sisters of Christ, her Son and liberator. Emphasis of the title "Mary as Mother" is found in early Carmelite writings, and in our own time. St. Thérèse of Lisieux said Mary for her was more mother than queen. Blessed

Titus Brandsma wrote that Carmelites by imitating Mary as Mother of Jesus — bring Jesus spiritually into today's world. Titus Brandsma used to say that St. John of the Cross is a Marian Doctor of the Church because his writings are concerned about how Christ is formed within us. Carmelites loved to compare the beauty of Mount Carmel with the spiritual beauty of Mary.

Carmelites recognized that it was the mother's task to conceive, nurture and foster life. Just as Mary brought Jesus into the world, so too, Carmelites are called to bring Jesus into the world. It is part of Carmelite contemplative prayer and ministry to continue that maternal task of Mary. To be other Jesus and Marys in the world, they must be united with both Jesus and Mary in mystical prayer and service.

For Carmelites the communal, ecclesial dimension of Mary's spiritual motherhood is of great importance. Both the Mother of Jesus and the beloved disciple stand larger than their private persons in their station at the cross on Calvary. Mary represents all believers and John represents all who need Mary to be mother and present Jesus to them. By the time Carmelites came on the scene, the truth of Mary's spiritual motherhood was well established, and our theologians and spiritual writings speak easily of Mary as Mother of all Carmelites.

Care must be taken not to interpret Mary's motherhood in a childish sense. There is nothing infantile about the notion of spiritual childhood of the Gospels or that of St. Thérèse of Lisieux. An awareness of being children of Mary is a corollary to the biblical teaching that we are children of God. Children in both cases emphasizes truths about ourselves (our needs, our weakness, our dignity) and also truths about God, our Creator and Redeemer, as well as about Mary who has been given to us by her Son.

The Scapular

One of the great symbols of Carmelite spirituality is the scapular. From the days when the Carmelites became European mendicants the scapular has been an important, though never exclusive, element of Carmelite attitudes towards Mary of Mount Carmel. This is so whether Mary be regarded as patroness, mother or virgin, model and sister to her Carmelite sisters and brothers. By way of the scapular the revered title of Mary, Our Lady of Mount Carmel, spread to the whole Church.

Among our authors of the past and in popular preaching, the scapular has been described as a sign of Mary's protection in life and death. The great promise embodied in the St. Simon Stock tradition concerns the gaining of eternal salvation — no one devoutly wearing the scapular of Mount Carmel will suffer damnation.

There are several legends in the Carmelite tradition concerning a vision of Our Lady giving the Scapular to the Order.[1] One such legend is that Our Lady appeared to Saint Simon Stock at Aylesford in England, another says she appeared in Oxford, yet another in Bordeaux. None of these can be verified. However, what is absolutely clear is that the Carmelites on Mount Carmel and when they came to Europe, were certain that they had a special relationship with Mary. They were convinced that she protected them because of their dedication to her. So they developed a strong symbol of this close relationship with Mary, which was a part of their clothing — a scapular, the sign that they and Mary were closely bound together, like a vassal wore the livery of his lord during the middle ages.

---

1 Carmelites today assess such visions, including the Scapular vision, according to two principal criteria established by Saint John of the Cross: (1) Visions are possible (The Ascent of Mount Carmel Bk. II, Ch. 16, Par. 3); (2) because visions, even if true, can mislead, it is better to renounce visions themselves, and take from them only the spirit of devotion to which they give rise (Ascent Bk. II, Ch. 17, Par. 9).

Some Carmelite writing and preaching has been exaggerated and superficial, but the solid tradition among Carmelite men and women has been both Christocentric and ecclesial.

Devotion to Mary's Carmelite scapular has no magic about it. It is worn as a sign that the devotee is turning to Mary in prayer expressing confidence in her motherly intercession. By wearing the scapular, we show the Catholic conviction that persevering in prayer is indeed a sign of salvation.

Scapular as Symbol

In order to understand the devotion to the scapular of Our Lady of Mount Carmel, we need to appreciate the meaning of symbols.[2] One model of symbols sees them in several stages.

The first stage of the symbols is the engendering experience which gives birth to the symbol; the second is a reflection on the symbol ; the third stage is a period when contact has been lost with the engendering experience, and the fourth stage is the need to invigorate the symbol anew.

All four stages can apply to the scapular. The first, the engendering experience, is the felt need of our Carmelite ancestors, which they found answered in God's love through the motherly mediation of Mary, mother and sister of all Carmelites, the Lady of the Manor, of their historical origins of Mount Carmel.

The scapular would never have become diffused in the Order unless its members resonated with and experienced the need of Mary's favor. In the initial experience, which we traditionally have associated with St. Simon Stock, a number of elements are found. Mary's role as Virgin mother, her favor to her children, her protection and intercession.

2 See: Carmelite Marian Commission: *Interim Report*, Rome, 1985, pp. 25-28.

In stage two the meaning of the symbols is spelt out for the adherents. For Carmelites, the 14th century brethren developed the scapular tradition in documents and traditions. One such is the sabbatine privilege — conveying the belief that Mary's protection extends even to purgatory. Reflections on the garment character of the scapular belong to this stage. This is when the scapular confraternities develop — sharing in the habit or sign of Carmelites' dedication to Mary.

In the third stage contact is often lost with the original experience. For the scapular the engendering experience involved many elements. The order had a patron to whom it owed dues and from whom it received favors. The order's patron was also mother and sister; most particularly perhaps it was a sense of its own and its members' need and Mary's protection. With the passing of time both the need and sense of Mary's response came to be simply repeated rather than reflected upon.

The final stage is the reinterpretation of the symbol. Today Carmelites are reflecting anew on the scapular tradition. The reconstruction of the symbol of the scapular comes not merely by study but by prayer. Experience of Mary and the Carmelites' relationship with her has to be born anew in the hearts of individuals and communities, with the scapular simply a sign of the Carmelites' devotion to Mary, seeing her as patroness, mother and sister. Those Catholics who wear the scapular or scapular medals simply share the Carmelites' love and relationship to Mary, the mother of the Church.

To appreciate the Marian charism we must know its origins, but for that charism to be living and productive we must integrate our history with what is best in contemporary biblical, liturgical and ecumenical perspectives. Mary is seen as the poor one of Nazareth, and is aligned with the poor and oppressed of the world. Mary of Mount Carmel is often revered by those who are alienated in many countries of the world. Through devotion to Mary, Carmelites reach out to those who need her protection, and those who used to hear Jesus' message of liberation. They imitate the motherhood of Mary, by bringing Jesus into the world of the poor, and model their life on their patroness, Mary, by hearing the cry of the poor. Part of the solemn blessing for the Feast of Our Lady of Mount Carmel in the present sacramentary reads: "Lord grant that those who in devotion have put on the habit of Our Lady of Mount Carmel may put on her virtues and enjoy her unfailing protection."

One of the great contributions of the pontificate of Pope John Paul II has been his reminder to the universal Church of the value of popular devotions. Devotion to Our Lady of Mount Carmel and the scapular is indeed very popular in many countries of the world. The challenge to the Carmelite Order is to support these popular devotions in local churches, while prophesying about abuses, superstitions, and magic which can take over. Encouragement of processions, icons, pilgrimages, statues, paintings, stained glass windows are all part of a pastoral realism which supports popular devotions like the scapular of Our Lady of Mount Carmel. There is a danger in multi-cultural societies like Australia and the USA that an Anglo-Celtic or sometimes an elitist Catholicism may dominate the local church. However, ethnic groups cannot be starved of genuine popular devotions which nourish their faith, life and culture.

The scapular as a potent image and symbol must be developed, renewed, and re-presented to the people of the local churches. Many countries of the world have virtually adopted Our Lady of Mount Carmel, so it is up to Carmelites to build on this love and to present our love of Mary, and our generative symbol, the scapular — as a solid part of Christian piety. It is also our challenge to present Mary as a genuine woman for today's world — a feminine charism basic to the full understanding of the Gospel message of Jesus. Again, Carmelites are among those Christians who prophesy against the demeaning and inequality of women which are part of the cultural and political structure of so many countries today.

Consequently, the generative symbol of the scapular of Our Lady of Mount Carmel reminds us of Mary — woman and mother, a reminder of the dignity and partnership of women, and the intercessory role of Mary in our liberation. The wearing of the scapular reminds us that Mary is aligned with the anawim — the poor and powerless of Christ.

In our devotion to Mary we are reminded that she is identified with her people in her fidelity, her poverty, her commitment. She is the teacher of contemplative prayer by her silence, her Magnificat and her standing beside the cross of Jesus. Her flight into Egypt allies her with the refugee, the voiceless and the most oppressed.

Mary and her scapular are symbols of reconciliation. Many places of pilgrimage bring people of all races, classes, and languages together. It means that all become poor pilgrims with Mary, and she challenges all to conversion and reconciliation not only with God, but with each other. It brings people into contact with the paschal mystery of Christ, the liberating work of Jesus.

Many present Mary in an elitist way. But a popular devotion, like the scapular has the power to integrate people, liberate them into the family of the liberated and reconciled. Popular Marian devotions can bring people to Jesus. Carmelites are called to build on the popular devotion to the scapular and to Our Lady of Mount Carmel by stressing Mary, the woman of the people, the woman who leads people to Jesus. All that Carmelites love and know about Mary can be handed on to the people through an authentic renewal of popular devotions.

The Marian charism of Carmelite spirituality is related to the prophetic charism, the inheritance of Elijah. Mary was seen by the early hermits as Queen of prophets. No one is more jealous than Mary for the rights of the true God. The message of Christianity gives the lie to human ideologies of omnipotence.

The closer God draws us to himself the more aware we become of our ignorance before mystery. The poverty and suffering of the world reflect the deeper hungers of the heart.

The biblical picture of Mary, the poor woman totally dependent on God, who lifts up the lowly, reminds us of our own need and sends us to God for help.

Masculine and Feminine

Carmelite spirituality, right from the inception of the tradition has maintained a balance between the masculine and feminine elements of humanity.

John Welch says that according to Carl Jung, every man has a feminine quality within him and every woman has a masculine quality within her.[3] Jung called the feminine element in a man the anima and the masculine element in a woman the animus. Jung describes the anima as that which sees relationships, makes whole, values and communicates, whereas the animus refers to the ability to discriminate, differentiate, define and rationalize.

These generalizations are difficult to make and sustain, but the experience of many men and women seems to agree that a fully mature man needs to develop and appreciate the feminine elements of his personality, and a fully mature woman the masculine elements of her personality. Consequently, men and women must have a healthy balance in their lives of the masculine and feminine side of their personalities. This balance leads to a union which many Carmelite writers have described in terms of marriage.

Spiritual marriage symbolizes the object of much of human longing for union with the other. The other can be seen as the

---

3 Welch, J., O.Carm., *Spiritual Pilgrims*, op. cit., pp. 166-170.

other in ourselves, the other human being, or the ultimate other who is God. The growth of each individual requires that the inner masculine or feminine figure be acknowledged, met and related to in genuine dialogue.

In choosing Elijah and Mary as their inspiration the original Carmelites were integrating the masculine and feminine elements of their lives. They have developed a spirituality which calls each man and woman who wants to follow Christ more fully to put into their lives the Elijah and Mary elements of the tradition. There are both the prophetic and the contemplative elements of life in Christ. For the Carmelite these elements must be present although in different proportions at different times of one's life.

For reflection: individuals or groups

1. What part does Mary play in your spiritual life?

2. What popular Marian devotions do you find helpful? What ones do you find unhelpful in your spiritual life?

3. Do you recognize a balance or an imbalance between the masculine and feminine elements of your personality? How do Jesus and Mary help you in this regard?

4. Is there an equal number of heroes and heroines in your life? What does this tell you about your personality and your spiritual experience?

Hints for writing and sharing:

See the end of the introduction

References used in Chapter 3

Carmelite Marian Commission: Interim Report. Rome, 1985.

Valabek, R., O.Carm., Mary, Mother of Carmel, Vol. II, Carmel in the World Paperbacks, Rome, 1988.

Welch, J., O.Carm., Spiritual Pilgrims. Paulist Press, New York, 1982.

_____ *Chapter   4* _____

St. Teresa of Avila,
Her Life and Spirit

St. Teresa of Avila, Spanish mystic, Doctor of the Church, Carmelite nun, is the greatest exponent of Carmelite spirituality. She is not only one of the heroines of the order, but one of the most influential figures in the post-reformation Church. Her spiritual doctrine, contained in her books and letters, built on the tradition of the medieval Carmelites, not only articulates clearly the Carmelite heritage, but adds to the corpus of spiritual writing and understanding in the Catholic Church. She not only helped to reform the Carmelite order, but contributed to the renewal of religious life and spirituality in the Church of her own age, and continues to influence the Church of the 20th century.

In this chapter we will look at her life, her times and writings, and come to a deeper understanding of Carmelite spirituality by looking at some of the symbols and images she used. Her main works are *Autobiography, The Way of Perfection, The Book of Foundations,* and *The Interior Castle.* For our purposes here we will concentrate on the last work, and examine the images of the "Castle," "water" and "journey." These images will not only help us learn more about the life of St. Teresa, but they will permit us to go more deeply into the heart and soul of Carmel.

Teresa de Cepeda y Ahumada was born in Avila on 28 March, 1515.[1] She grew up in a happy family and was the third child of the second marriage of Don Alonso Sanchez de Cepeda with Doña Beatriz de Ahumada. When she left home to join religious life, it caused her great suffering to leave her father's house. In 1535 she joined the Carmelite convent of the Incarnation in Avila. The atmosphere of this convent was a busy one, but in no way was it dissolute or immoral. One hundred and eighty nuns lived there and enclosure was not very strict. Teresa lived with many outstanding religious and met many devout Carmelite friars and priests from other Orders. Teresa says that all the religious observances in force in those days were faithfully kept. However, she began to feel a call to a more simple and more enclosed form of Carmelite life.

Teresa's father, Alonso, died on 24 December, 1543. This proved to be a difficult time for her; "In losing him I was losing every good and joy, and he was everything to me. . . ." At the same time she had been living her religious life in a certain amount of conflict. She wrote:

> I voyaged on this tempestuous sea for almost 20 years with these fallings and risings and this evil — since I fell again — and all life so beneath perfection that I paid almost no attention to venial sins. And mortal sins, although I feared them, I did not fear them as I should have since I did not turn away from the dangers. I should say that it is one of the most painful lives, I think, that one can imagine; for neither did I enjoy God nor did I find happiness in the world. When I was experiencing the enjoyments of the world, I felt sorrow when I recalled what I owed God. When I was with God, my

---

1 For historical details I rely on: Smet, J., O.Carm., *The Carmelites*, Vol. II, Carmelite Spiritual Center, Darien, IL, 1976, pp. 22-93.

attachments to the world disturbed me. This is a war so
troublesome that I don't know how I was able to suffer it even
a month, much less for so many years (*Autobiography*, Ch. 8).[2]

Teresa was in the convent for about 20 years and 39 years
of age when she underwent a kind of conversion, which led her
to a closer relationship with God. She had been reading the
Confessions of St. Augustine, "When I came to the passage where
he speaks about his conversion and read how he heard voices in
the garden, it only seemed to me, according to what I felt in my
heart, that it was I the Lord called" (*Autobiography*, Ch. 8).

Teresa, some fellow Carmelites, and some of her relatives
discussed the idea of opening their own reformed Carmelite
convent. Teresa felt that prayer, solitude and simplicity of life
which were the traditional hallmarks of Carmel suffered at the
convent of the Incarnation. The insufficient income for a large
number of nuns led to the breakdown of the common life, and
the development of class distinctions among the community, as
the nuns were forced to fend for themselves. This prompted
Teresa to desire a more prayerful and less distracted form of
religious life.

The Carmelites, prior to 1562, were living according to an
adapted Rule of St. Albert. She wanted to return to the "primitive" rule of Carmel. St. Teresa thought the rule as adapted by
Innocent IV in 1247 was the first and primitive rule. The rule of
St. Albert given to the hermits on Mount Carmel about 1206-
1214 was in fact the unchanged and primitive rule. Be that as it
may, it is clear that St. Teresa wanted to live the Carmelite life in
imitation of the hermits on Mount Carmel. In order to do this in
16th century Spain she had to be, like the early Carmelites,
creative in her thinking.

2 Translation: Kavanaugh, K., OCD, and Rodriguez, O., OCD, *The Collected Works of Saint
Teresa of Avila*, Vol. I, ICS Publications, Washington, DC. 1976, pp. 94-95.

Teresa's reform of Carmelite life gradually became a reality with the opening of the Convent of St. Joseph in Avila in 1562. The nuns of the first reformed convent were to be no more than 13, they shared all in common with no personal servants as there had been in the Incarnation. St. Teresa developed a community life which came close to the hermitical life of the first Carmelites on Mount Carmel.

She was encouraged wholeheartedly by the Prior General of the Carmelite order, John Rossi. From 1566-1570 she founded seven more reformed convents and before she died she had founded 14 convents. The saint envisioned her convents as castles of prayer fueling the work of the counter reformation Church both in Europe and in the Spanish new world. Through her relationship with St. John of the Cross the reform took hold among the friars. She died in 1582 revered by the Carmelites and all of Spain as a great saint.

The Interior Castle [3]

The book St. Teresa called *The Interior Castle* is very much her spiritual story. By using symbols and her imagination, Teresa takes us into her soul, and tells us about her relationship with God. Her story centers on a castle which is like a crystal globe. She calls the soul, or the person, the main character of the story, and the person is invited to begin a journey to the very center of the castle, where she says, the King lives.

The atmosphere around the castle is cold and dark, the surrounding land is unpleasant and crawling with snakes and various dangerous creatures. As the person enters the castle the darkness gives way to light and glow and warmth seem to come

---

3 For the way St. Teresa uses the symbols of "castle," "water," "journey," I follow the work of: Welch, J., O.Carm., *op. cit.*, Chs. 2, 3 and 4.

from the interior. To get to the King one has to move through various rooms. These rooms are arranged in concentric circles St. Teresa calls dwelling places which have rooms above, below and beside each other.

The first dwelling place consists of all the rooms on the surface of the globe. There are seven dwelling places which are milestones on the journey to the center of the castle, the seventh being the center itself.

For St. Teresa, each dwelling place in her castle is a world itself, containing rooms, gardens, fountains and passageways. Each of these places has its own attractions for the traveller, but the strongest attraction comes from the center.

This is Teresa's description of her relationship with God and, more particularly, her life of prayer. She is telling us her story by the images of journeying into this huge crystal castle to seek the King as its center. Prayer is her door to the castle and prayer draws her through the various dwellings to the chamber of the King. The saint's relationship with God is described as she experienced the delights, peace, tension, satisfaction, frustration, emptiness and the growth of coming closer to God.

The first three places in the castle describe the efforts people make when they begin a serious prayer relationship with God. St. Teresa calls this meditation or active prayer. In the first dwelling the person experiences a call from God to embark on a journey which will bring him or her closer to Him. This person has begun a prayer life. However, St. Teresa says that the unpleasant darkness and the creatures outside the castle tend to get into these places. So there are many distractions which draw the person away from moving closer to the center and consequently closer to God.

St. Teresa describes this stage:

"Even though they may not be a bad state, they are involved in worldly things and so absorbed with its possessions, honors

or business affairs, that even though they would want to see
and enjoy its beauty these things do not allow them to; nor
does it seem that they can slip free from so many impediments." (*Interior Castle*, I,Ch. 2, No. 14.) [4]

Although the journey has begun, the person is torn by many
things and finds attention to prayer difficult in this first dwelling
place.

In the second place, or concentric layer of rooms, St. Teresa
says people hear the call of God in a more personal way. This is a
personal challenge, where they enter a deeper relationship with
God calling for greater efforts in the spiritual life. Teresa describes this by saying that hearing his voice is a greater trial than
not hearing it. This often disorientates and destabilizes people,
by putting them off-center so that they will be challenged to get
their priorities right.

The third place is a time of greater interior peace. Prayer
becomes a part of the daily life of the sincere person who is
seeking a closer relationship with God. St. Teresa says that there
are many adults who are in this state. These people are living
fairly stable and orderly lives, putting prayer and the sacraments
high on their list and reaching out to be of service to their
brethren.

Some people find the third place comfortable and satisfy-
ing, but others feel a call to move deeper into the castle. This call
often comes by no longer finding the prayer of the third dwelling
satsifying. God seems to destabilize the person again, and many
people misinterpret the signs. They tend to think there is
something wrong with them because they no longer find consolation in prayer and fulfillment in their spiritual life. Teresa
shows us that there is in fact nothing wrong with the sincere
person, but God is calling them to another form of prayer and

4 Translation: Kavanaugh, K., OCD, and Rodriguez, O., OCD, *op. cit.*, Vol. II, p. 294.

different kind of spiritual relationship. God wants them to let go of the stability they felt in the third dwelling place.

The fourth dwelling, for St. Teresa, is a period of change. The person is called from an active prayer to a more passive form of prayer, which she calls the prayer of quiet. To distinguish between active meditation used in the first three dwelling places and the prayer of quiet of the fourth place, St. Teresa uses the metaphors of two troughs of water. The first is filled with great efforts by means of aqueducts, while the second is filled quickly and easily from a spring. The first trough is active meditation and the second is the prayer of quiet.

St. Teresa says that the fifth dwelling is a time for consolidation of passive prayer which becomes, in her terms, the prayer of union. She describes this form of prayer which a person does not understand because the union with God is always short and brief. It is like dying with Christ and rising with him to a new life.

The sixth dwelling place is a symbol for a deepening of contemplative prayer and the prayer of union. This can be a time of decentering of a person with many challenges, and interior and exterior trials. Teresa characterizes this time of her life like a betrothal and preparation for marriage. It is a night of the spirit which brings many sufferings into the spiritual life of the pilgrim journeying to the center of the castle.

She described her experience of God in prayer in this dwelling like a fire in her heart.

> "I do know that it seems this pain reaches to the soul's very depths and that when the one who wounds it draws out the arrow, it indeed seems in accord with the deep love that the soul feels that God is drawing these very depths after him." (*Interior Castle*, VI, Ch. 2, No. 4.) [5]

5 *Ibid.* p. 368.

In the seventh dwelling place there is a transforming communion with God. At the center of the castle St. Teresa spoke of an intellectual vision of the Trinity, and an imaginative vision of Jesus which brings the inner journey to a conclusion. She describes this union like rain falling into a river — the union of the water is complete. Paradoxically, the arrival at the center of the castle propels a person to greater commitment to the needs of people.

> "This is the reason for prayer, my daughters, the purpose of this spiritual marriage: the birth always of good works, good works." (*Interior Castle*, VII, Ch. 4, No. 6.) [6]

The Images of Teresa

In *The Interior Castle* St. Teresa describes her story by using a number of impressive images, which draw people to a deeper understanding of their lives. She used these images because she found it difficult to describe her relationship with God in any other form of language. For her, the experiences of her prayer are close to inexpressible, so she tries to give a psychological description of her own life. The journey to God in the center of the castle is also a journey into the center of oneself. These are really one journey to her, implying that God is at the very center of a person's life.

These images are not simply means of telling a story, they are powerful and generative in that they come very close to describing the very mystery of life. They generate in people who read St. Teresa an understanding of their own personal journey to God and to the center of their being. They help us to find images for our own story. For some who study depth psychology

6 *Ibid.* p. 446.

and imagery, St. Teresa has expressed for all people a collective experience, so that her explanations can move us who are far removed from this 16th century Spanish cloistered nun. St. Teresa's story can become our story and her images can lead us into our own center where God awaits us.

The castle image calls us to the center of our lives, water speaks to the hidden depths which hold much of our life. Journey shows us that we are pilgrims who have to meet the changes and movements which are part of our development in the spiritual life.

Water

The second provocative symbol used by St. Teresa is water. In *The Interior Castle* she said that she has not found anything more appropriate to explain some spiritual experiences than water. We have already seen how she explains the difference between active meditation and the prayer of quiet by the symbol of water getting into the two troughs.

The trough which is filled by aqueducts is the metaphor for the prayer that begins with the person and ends in God. With God's grace, the person begins the effort and with a use of imagination, reflection and prayer sustained it. The other trough that is filled from the spring symbolizes prayer that begins with God and ends with the person. It is little to do with our own efforts and comes from the infusion of the Holy Spirit. God is the source of this water, which is the experience of the person in the fourth dwelling place.

Although St. Teresa continues the water imagery in the sixth dwelling she expands her metaphors.

It seems that the trough of water we mentioned (I believe it was in the fourth dwelling, for I don't recall exactly) filled so easily and gently, I mean without any movement. Here this great God, who holds back the springs of water and doesn't allow the sea to go beyond its boundaries, opens the springs from which the water in this trough flows. With a powerful impulse, a huge wave rises up so forcefully that it lifts high this little bark that is our soul. A bark cannot prevent the furious waves from leaving it where they will; nor does the pilot have the power, nor do those who take part in controlling the little ship. (*Interior Castle*, VI, Ch. 5, No. 3.) [7]

When St. Teresa uses water as an image, she wants to explain the sense of the riches at the very center of the human person. Her use of water attempts to express psychologically the experience of her relationship with God in prayer. Water expresses her awareness of the presence of God in the center of her spirit. St. Teresa is an early psychologist attempting to articulate the effect of the action of God in her life. Water helps express the depths of human interiority.

What happens when the water dries up? [8] Or when there is a drought? Some people find that they can no longer pray like they could before, and they have no consolations in prayer. People, then, often think they have failed God in some way or that they may have displeased him, or that they have been negligent. But after sincere examination if they find that they have not failed God in any way, St. Teresa explains what may have happened. Through the image of water, she says that God often causes a lack of water, a dryness or a drought so that people will move onto the next stage of prayer and the spiritual life. Our experience of dryness in prayer is not merely a frustrating experience of the absence of God. It is an essential experience of

7 *Ibid.* p. 387.
8 For a longer answer to this question see: Green, T.H., SJ, *When the Well Runs Dry*, Ave Maria Press, Notre Dame, IN, 1979, pp. 81-96.

our identification with Jesus who "learned obedience through suffering" (Heb 5:8). The Lord's ways are not ours, and he demands that we leave all to follow him. He calls us forward to the center through a journey which often means identifying with the abandoned Jesus. In this way we come closer to God at the center and at our center.

We must let go and allow him to take over where we shall go. The mysterious meaning of the spiritual life is that in losing ourselves we find Jesus — it's the paradox of the whole Christian life — when I lose my life, I find it. St. Teresa has explained this like a masterful teacher of the spiritual life.

Journey

St. Teresa has developed the ancient Carmelite image of journey or pilgrimage. The early Carmelites saw themselves as pilgrims who had literally journeyed to the Holy Land to find Jesus Christ. St. Teresa has picked up this image and developed it to mean the interior journey to which God calls each person to help find themselves and to discover God. The person wanting to find Christ is called to make a pilgrimage to their center where the human and divine meet.

The basic model for the Christian pilgrimage is the Way of the Cross. That is the pre-eminent journey to the center. However, all pilgrims are called to leave their familiar world where they are secure. Pilgrims become displaced persons, where one's normal routines and relationships are absent. Like the crucified Christ, pilgrims become the poor and the marginalized. They are stripped of their familiar clothing so they may be more attentive to the call of the God at the center. However, pilgrims are the liberated ones, freed from daily preoccupations and unnecessary baggage in order to contemplate their Lord and to attend to the poor and oppressed they meet on the way.

St. Teresa has reminded us that to be a pilgrim on a journey we must be identified with the rejected and crucified Christ. She has also reminded spiritual pilgrims that to find the crucified Christ, they must seek him in those who are being crucified — rejected, oppressed — in our world. So pilgrims must be identified with the oppressed and learn, know and love the Christ they see in their lives. In her writings St. Teresa had a trilogy of humility, poverty and fraternity which recalled to her the hermit-pilgrim-mendicant brothers of Mount Carmel. She recognized that to find Christ at the center of one's soul one had to experience the humility and poverty of the least of God's creatures. She teaches us today that without solidarity with the poorest of the poor in real fraternity, we will never find the crucified one, nor experience his resurrection.

St. Teresa and Prayer

Segundo Galilea[9] says that St. Teresa offers us a synthesis between contemplative prayer and commitment to our brothers and sisters. For St. Teresa true prayer is not only inseparable from true commitment, but is performed in the practice of charity.

For St. Teresa the essence of sanctity is the practice of conformity with the will of God. For her the value of prayer derives from the love with which it is made, and the practice of love to which it leads. Conformity with the will of God consists in the practice of fraternal love motivated by the fact that Jesus lives in others. She used to tell her nuns that true perfection is the love of God and our neighbor, and that the surest sign that we are keeping these two commandments is our love for others.

St. Teresa insists that the life of prayer always be nourished

9 Galilea, S., the Future of Our Past, Ave Maria Press, Notre Dame, IN, 1985.

by the humanity of Christ. The humanity of Jesus is the only way to the Father and to the demands of the kingdom. Above all she recommended contemplation on the sufferings of Jesus. For her, the devotion to the passion was irreplaceable, since the experience had shown her that it provided the most realistic barrier against false mysticism. It was the best way to encourage the imitation of Christ. In the humanity of Christ, she found a balance and realism in contemplative prayer. Here again, we see St. Teresa relying on and developing the early medieval Carmelite tradition. As we have seen earlier, the Rule of St. Albert insisted that the following of Jesus Christ is fundamental to Carmelite life, and his death and resurrection are central to Carmelite spirituality. So it is with Teresa.

In *The Way of Perfection*,[10] Teresa says that the Gospels were the source of her sustenance in prayer and were practically the only book she used. Her love of Jesus, and her vocation to follow him formed the very basis of her life. Even when she had mystical experiences, she still prized the closeness of the human Jesus as vitally important. When she explained to her fellow Carmelites the challenge of poverty, love in the community, chastity and fidelity she reminded them of Jesus and his purity or singleness of heart.

Concentrating on the sufferings of Jesus brings the disciple's attention to the sufferings of so many people in the world. Jesus had a special love for the oppressed and the alienated, so attention to his suffering in prayer brings us into solidarity with the poor. It brings our attention to the need for prophetism and martyrdom. The prophet, who aligns himself/herself with the oppressed, will have to face, like Jesus, the martyrdom of rejection and even physical death. The persecution, passion and martyrdom of Jesus, Galilea explains, will always be the most

10 Kavanaugh, K., OCD, and Rodriguez, O., OCD, *op. cit.*, Vol. II, p. 118.

radical model of Christian commitment, as well as the cost of Christian discipleship.

For St. Teresa, meditation on the rejection, sufferings, death and resurrection of Jesus, brings realism and hope to prayer and apostolate. She saw that Jesus had to be at the center of our prayer-life and our ministerial life. For her, prayer nourished the apostolate and the apostolate nourished our prayer. Our closeness to Christ in prayer raises our consciousness to sin and evil. We become more aware of our personal sin and our need for Christ to forgive us and reconcile us to the Father. But our prayer also makes us aware of sin and its evil effects in the world — whether it be in our religious communities or our social organizations. This is why the sufferings and death of Jesus always need to be one with the resurrection. If we leave out the risen Christ we tend to be overwhelmed by the hopelessness of evil in our lives and in the world.

Consequently, the practice of asceticism, for St. Teresa, is part of this prayer life concentrating on Jesus. We need ascetic practices to keep us close to the commands of the kingdom, and not to be seduced by the evils of the world. In our society St. Teresa would warn us against consumerism, matrialism, the gap between rich and poor, the paying of unjust wages, the lack of creative work, the lack of sharing in power. Today we need a prayer calling us to asceticism and a struggle against evil in solidarity with those suffering from these evils. This requires abnegation and self-discipline. It is pointless, for example, to criticize the consumer society if we ourselves (individually and as communities) do not consume less and embrace poverty. It is useless to deplore the plight of the poor, unless we enter into solidarity with them, which involves many renunciations.

It is the doctrine of St. Teresa on prayer which has called us to realism and hope. She has helped us to seek Christ by entering the castle, by watching the garden of love and by journeying like simple pilgrims to Christ at the center of our lives. St. Teresa is as relevant today as she was in 16th century Spain, because she has had the ability to universalize her own experience of God in prayer. She has articulated Carmelite spirituality and made it available to more people throughout the ages.

For reflection: individuals or groups

1. How do you describe prayer in your life? What images and metaphors do you use? (St. Teresa used "the journey inward," or "water," or going into a "castle.")

2. What do your images tell you about your prayer in your life?

3. How do the liturgy and the sacraments help you to pray?

Hints for writing and sharing:

See the end of the introduction

References used in Chapter 4

Galilea, S., The Future of Our Past. Ave Maria Press, Notre Dame, IN, 1985.

Green, T.H., SJ., When the Well Runs Dry. Ave Maria Press, Notre Dame, IN, 1979.

Smet, J., O.Carm., The Carmelites, Vol. II. Carmelite Spiritual Center, Darien, IL, 1976.

Welch, J., O.Carm., Spiritual Pilgrims. Paulist Press, NY, 1982.

St. John of the Cross, the Poet

John de Yepes was born at Fontiveros in central Spain on 24 June, 1542.[1] He was 27 years younger than St. Teresa of Avila. His father, Gonzalo de Yepes came from a noble family, but he was disowned by them when he married a girl beneath his rank, Catalina Alvarez. Gonzalo took up his wife's craft of weaving, but died soon after John's birth. Catalina was obliged to support her three sons by her own labor. Hence in 1551 Catalina moved to Medina del Campo, a large town with better chances of finding work. Here John experienced a loving family life which, though simple, bordered on poverty. At the age of 21, John entered the convent of the Carmelite friars in Medina del Campo, taking the name of John of St. Matthias.

After a year's novitiate he was sent to the Carmelite student house at Salamanca where from 1564 to 1568 he attended the famous university. In the year 1567 St. John was ordained, five

---

1 For the historical facts see: Smet, J., O.Carm., *The Carmelites*, Vol. II, Carmelite Spiritual Center, Darien, IL, 1976, pp. 127-130.

years after St. Teresa had established the first convent of reformed Carmelite nuns. Both St. Teresa and the Prior General,
John Baptist Rossi (called Rubeo by the Spaniards), were anxious
to have some contemplative Carmelite friars to minister to the
nuns of the reform. She asked the prior of the Carmelites in
Medina for some friars who would follow the reform.

Consequently, the first friars of the reformed Carmel
established their convent at Duruelo on 28 November, 1568.
The Father Provincial of Castile offered Mass and received their
vows made according to the Rule of St. Albert of 1247. The first
friars were the prior of the Carmelite Convent of Medina del
Campo, Fray Anthony of Jesus, John de Yepes, who changed his
title from "of St. Matthias" to "of the Cross," and a deacon,
Joseph of Christ. The Provincial clothed them in the reformed
Carmelite habit of rough undyed wool and they discarded their
shoes. This later earned them the nickname of Discalced which
has stuck throughout history.

St. Teresa worked hard with the support of the Prior
General and other Church officials to spread the reform among
the Carmelite order. St. John of the Cross took a less active role,
but nevertheless earned the admiration of all as a faithful religious, renowned confessor and spiritual director. In 1572 we
find St. John of the Cross and Germain of St. Matthias as
confessors to the convent of the Incarnation at Avila. Due to
raucous rows, which seem incredible to our 20th century ears,
the two friars were forcibly removed from the convent and
imprisoned — this happened late in 1577. St. John of the Cross
was held captive in the Carmelite convent in Toledo from which
he escaped in August 1578.

The importance of this incident has been blown out of all
proportion. Biographers and novelists have spared neither
imagination nor descriptive skill on the story of St. John's
capture and treatment in prison. The historical fact is that little

first hand information is available. Not all the punishments applicable by law are to be presumed to have been applied to all prisoners. Imprisonment, flogging, fasting on bread and water were standard penalties in religious orders of the period, Discalced Carmelites as well as others. This is not to deny the accused were treated unjustly and with severity because religious disputes at that time inflamed strong feelings and behaviors.

One bright ray in this dark picture of poor behavior was that in his prison cell in Toledo St. John of the Cross composed a number of his greatest works, including most of *The Spiritual Canticle*, some poems, and *The Dark Night*. And to give St. John his due he had enough gumption and common sense to escape from his prison cell in the summer of 1578.

Although St. John did not take much part in actively spreading the reform he was extremely influential as one of the founding friars, from the character of his writings and poetry, and his unquestioned sanctity. Others, like Fray Nicholas (Doria) and Fray Jerome (Gracian), took a more active role in the struggles and unbelievable arguments of the early years of the reform. St. John was several times elected prior, definitor and consultor. Apart from some letters mostly dating from the last years of the saint's life, primary sources contemporary to events are scarce.

At the chapter of 1591, St. John retired from all offices and wanted to live simply in Andalucia, his favorite place on earth. On 21 September St. John wrote to a friend, "Tomorrow I go to Ubeda to cure a slight bout of fever, for as I have been suffering from it daily for over a week, I think I need medical aid; but I go with the intention of returning here again, for in truth I am deriving great good from this holy retreat." After painful and useless surgery, St. John of the Cross died at Ubeda on 14 December 1591. Both St. John and St. Teresa died as members of the Carmelite Order, because it was only after their deaths others decided to form a completely separate Order, the

Discalced Carmelites. He was canonized in 1726 and declared a
doctor of the universal Church by Pope Pius XI in 1926. St. John
of the Cross' feast day is 14 December.

St. John, the Poet

Much attention has been given to St. John's prose writings
as classical explanations of a prayerful relationship with God.
However, St. John's prose is shot through with rich imagery
which seems to be the only vehicle he can find to explain what he
wants to say. The key to understanding St. John's contribution to
Carmelite spirituality is to see him as a sublime poet.

Evelyn Woodward [2] has noted that the poet lives with a
sensitivity which is open to the nuances of life and the vagaries of
the human spirit. Poets share their perceptions and heightened
awareness in language and metaphor. They hear, see and speak
in ways many of us cannot. They are the ones who contemplate
rather than do, they see value rather than utility, they evoke
rather than analyze, they point rather than grasp, they dream
rather than plan.

The moods of poets illuminate what many see only dimly;
they strip away our illusions, masks and pretensions, leaving us
exposed and vulnerable. Poetry arises from contemplation and
silence. T.S. Eliot says that poets are alone and often prone to
suffering brought about by their super sensitivity. Poets see
beyond themselves, but are aware of their own inner life and
experience, and so emphathize and generalize from it.

2 Woodward, E . *Poets, Prophets and Pragmatists*, Collins Dove, Blackburn, Vic., 1987, pp.
   12-16.

"O Night which was my guide,
O Night fairer than dawn,
O Night which to the side
of lover brought his bride
And then did make them one!
I stayed: he let me rest
My cheek upon his breast . . ." [3]
(*The Dark Night I*)

As poet, mystic and contemplative the soul of St. John leapt into rapturous heights. He finds it difficult to use ordinary language to describe his relationship to God and often uses the analogy of bride and bridegroom. His imagination uses the colors and patterns of symbolic language even to the point where he confessed that he scarcely knew what he was saying. Poems like his cannot be simply analyzed in a rational way, but listened to as one listens to a melody of Mozart. His poems have a strange dreamlike quality. His poetry is like a metaphysical fire — a kind of white heat which touches our very souls.

One dark night
Fired with love's urgent longings
— Ah, the sheer grace —
I went out unseen,
My house being now all stilled. [4]
(En una noche obscura,
Con ansias en amores inflamada,
Oh dichosa ventura
Sali sin ser notada
Estando ya mi casa sosegada.)

3 Translation: Peers, A., as quoted in Sencourt, R., *Carmelite and Poet*, Hollis and Carter, London, 1943, p. 120.
4 Translation: Kavanaugh, K., OCD, and Rodriguez, O., OCD, *The Collected Works of Saint John of the Cross*, ICS Publications, Washington, DC, 1979, p. 711.

In his poetry there is an abandonment to love which is based on the spiritual longing and desire to be united with God. The harmonies and colors of the poems convey their own meaning and sense. St. John shows his ecstasy of love when meeting the mysteries of Christ.

Thomas Merton says the poet is an innocent.[5] There is no magic of words in the poet "only life in all its unpredictability and all its freedom." Thus, the freedom of the poet is to remain outside the temporal imprisonments of institutional living and to span past, present and future, bringing the light of what is best in history to bear on the struggles in the present and pointing to the unknown future with hope and love.

> "O woods and thickets,
> Planted by the hand of the Beloved!
> O meadow of verdure, enamelled with flowers,
> Says if he has passed by you."

St. John, the poet, being a person of discernment, was sensitive to the injustices and exaggerations of his time, and in his innocence he made people aware of them. Poets are uncomfortable people to be with. Certainly, toward the end of his life those with power did not want him close to them. St. John, the poet, called on his fellow religious to examine stagnation in their lives and institutions — he did this by the force of the sanctity of his life and the power of his poetry. He was a silent contemplative who suffered, not only because of his own empathy, but because he threatened the powerful. Out of his silence he caressed and challenged all who read his poetry.

---

5 Merton, T., *Raids on the Unspeakable*, New Directions, New York, NY, 1966, p. 159.

St. John of the Cross and Freedom

Does St. John of the Cross speak of the problem of freedom and alienation experienced by modern people? If so, is his teaching theologically valid for us today?

Freedom is often mentioned in the Sanjuanist literature. [6]

David Centner believes that the whole frame of reference for the discussion of freedom is the journey inward to the center of the person's being. The main analogy which St. John uses to explain his teaching is that of flight and rendezvous by night. The symbol of night is so powerful that we often overlook the element of movement in the analogy. Much of John's teaching on liberation makes sense only by reference to the motion of the inner person ("the soul" in St. John's terminology) in its journey toward union with its beloved.

In his writing St. John of the Cross frequently uses comparisons which indicate various kinds of possibilities and impossibilities. Sometimes the saint uses figures of speech which are often logical, referring to freedom and alienation. For example: "Joy is blinding to the heart and does not allow it to consider and ponder things . . ."; and, "The third sign . . . is the powerlessness . . . to meditate."

Again, in Carmelite spirituality we see the basic journey image. This is found in many of the references to impede activity, though not every motion word is directly applicable to the basic analogy. For example, we find the term "to turn back" in chapter 8 of the 1st Book of the Night and it seems to be an ordinary figure of speech, similar to the English expression "to backslide."

Even though we may not be sure how a term is to be

---

6 This section has been assisted by the research of Centner, D., OCD, "Christian Freedom and the Nights of Saint John of the Cross" in Sullivan, J., OCD (Ed.), *Carmelite Studies*, Vol. 2, ICS Publications, Washington, DC, 1982.

interpreted, the fact remains that St. John's language relies heavily on the analogical use of words referring to motion and physical freedom.

Among the most frequently used terms are: "to hinder," "impede," "to grasp and let go of." Less common are the words, "to obstruct" and "to detain" and their cognates. The word "slavery" and its synonyms are surprisingly rare in contrast with "freedom" and its related forms. The saint often reinforces the meaning of the above words by combining them with substantives which turn them into more extended analogies. Examples of these include: "snare," "capture," "injury" (probably the most common) "obstacle" and "prison." Sometimes words indicating the impeding of motion are used to refer to some psychological activity.

If we develop this thought, many terms which are not directly related to freedom or slavery acquire a relationship through the contexts surrounding them. These are mainly descriptions of the states of the person and include: "nakedness," "poverty," "solitude," and "emptiness."

Frequently St. John uses the analogy of physical impediment and personal freedom in extended metaphors. The most famous ones are that of the bird held captive by a thread, and another in the comparison of the dulling of reason with the wine of Babylon and the enslavement of Samson by his enemies.

Much can be learned from St. John of the Cross' use of symbol and metaphor. However, it does not necessarily follow that he intends to examine what we call the problem of freedom and alienation in the 20th century. Theologians have shown that in fact the teaching of St. John of the Cross is theologically and psychologically very relevant for us today.

Ruth Burrows says that the whole aim of St. John of the Cross is to release us from the tyranny of the ego.[7] When we

7 Burrows, R., *Ascent to Love*, Dimension Books, Denville, NJ, 1987, pp. 37-48.

keep looking at Jesus, we make our choices in line with the values of Jesus. He continually calls us to transcend ourselves and to keep reaching for the Father by a denial of our self sufficiency which comes from the prompting and the limitations of our ego.

The power of our ego leads us to make ourselves the center of our own universe. While we all have basic human rights to protect and promote, there is a danger that we will be overwhelmed by a selfish notion of our own self-importance. St. John says that if you want to love God, if you want to begin to ascend the mountain, you must choose against your own self-importance. You have to take yourself out of the spotlight, and see yourself as a member of a community whom you are meant to serve. The sincere followers of Jesus must wish to become the servant of all and not the center of attention.

The drive of the ego often brings an enslavement to human respect where we are ruled by what others think of us. St. John says that we must be freed from this slavery if we want to love God in contemplation. As a servant of all, or thinking little of ourselves, we are not likely to be interested in the frailties of our neighbor and thus be the sort of person who will sit in judgment of others. In the writings of St. John he says that when we free ourselves from the tyranny of the ego, the slavery of self-importance, we begin to experience the refreshment of the Holy Spirit. This comes in the form of the infused theological virtues of faith, hope and love. These gifts from God help us to make right judgments, because a person overcome by selfishness cannot make the correct decisions.

The mystical journey up the side of the mountain of Carmel in the darkness of night is a liberation because it is an effective means of attaining, insofar as it is possible in this life, to the perfection of one's being in a union of love centered in Christ between the human person and God. St. John shows us by being freed from the obstacles to union, which also are the obstacles to holiness, we reach our final transformation, our final freedom.

Christians are attracted and impelled by God's love, and so we begin actively to enter into the night of the senses through Christ-centered choices which unite our psychological and spiritual energies and help us to focus on our true vocation — union with God. People's efforts would be unable to achieve anything more than moral self-improvement were it not for the fact that they are sustained by the gracious intervention of the Holy Spirit, the theological virtues of faith, hope and love.

St. John in scholastic language, and today's theologians, explain that these virtues allow people to know and love God and to begin to choose him in himself. This choice for God is not simply built on the natural goodness in people, but on the transcendental graciousness of God. Love, especially in its intuitive and erotic aspect, directs the person's energies toward God in an increasingly inclusive concern, or unconditional love. As people begin to choose in this transcendental manner, they become more and more God-centered, and by their choices they begin to liberate themselves from the impediments which block their journey. By means of the theological virtues, the Lord begins to introduce the person to what St. John calls the night of the spirit, a kind of dark contemplation.

In this dark contemplation when we cooperate with the Spirit we begin to choose God without too much effort. The attraction of God's love and our response bring about a renunciation which detaches us from purely natural responses, and re-orders our concern for them as part of the all-inclusive love of God and his creation. As this contemplation penetrates ever more deeply into the depth of our personalities, we gain a certain dominion over our drives and appetites. Our love of God grows with its own passion, and we come to love God with the strength of our whole person. This work of the Holy Spirit in the heart of people frees them from the defensive way of using their powers: perceptions, feelings and intellect. At this stage people develop an acute consciousness of their own defects, finiteness, and smallness in the sight of God, who often feels absent from them. God also frees people from their false notion of who God is and what he does in their lives and in the world. This is a liberation which allows people to surrender lovingly to God and do his work in the Church and the world. This letting go is described by St. John like a death, whereby we cease to live our own life, but God lives his life in us and through us. St. John sees this as linking the person intimately to the death and resurrection of Jesus. Here we see the Carmelite stress on the paschal mystery, and the Christocentric nature of the Carmelite vocation as seen in the writings of the medieval Carmelites.

Personal sins and the sin of the world have no longer domination over the person in the state of liberation, and he/she lives for God and what God wishes to achieve in the world. These people of the Lord have effected a final freedom in this life by accepting from God the gift of his self-bestowal in a loving union. St. John teaches that the ultimate liberation is our natural death, by which we fly directly to a waiting and loving God.

The Dark Night

One of the most striking images in the writings of St. John of the Cross is his use of the symbolism of the night. The Dark Night has the lover wandering around in the dark seeking the lost beloved. All people who seek a close relationship with God have to experience in one way or another a dark night of both the senses and the spirit. After the experience of the night there is the introduction to the light of a new day. [8]

St. John uses his imagery to describe the situation of people who have begun the spiritual life well and have been rather

---

8 This is explained very clearly by Green, T.H., SJ, *When the Well Runs Dry*, Ave Maria Press, Notre Dame, IN, 1979, pp. 114-129.

successful in coming in contact with God. They experience
many consolations and feel very close to God in prayer. However, after a while their prayer and concerns for the things of
God seem to strike a dryness which St. John calls a dark night.
They cannot seem to find God in prayer any more and they feel
abandoned by God.

This experience is recognized, St. John tells us, by the
presence of three signs. He says that this darkness in our spiritual
life could be due to our own negligence or sinfulness or sickness.
He says there are three signs which tell us that this darkness is
really the work of God in our lives.

The first sign is that while people do not find consolation in
prayer and the things of God, they also do not find any consolation in other pursuits. Many people turn from prayer to enjoy-
ment to try to brighten up their lives. However, this proves to be
pretty dark also. But St. John says this sign alone is not enough.
The second sign is that people's memories are ordinarily
centered on God, with painful care, thinking that they are not
serving God. People find themselves in an ambiguous situation
by wanting to be near God, but not being able to find him. This
is frustrating, because people say they are miserable without
him. The third sign St. John gives is the inability to meditate
with the imagination as one was used to do with some facility.

> He writes that the person, "can no longer meditate and make
> use of the imagination . . . as was one's previous custom. At
> this time God does not communicate himself to the person
> through the senses as he did before . . . but by pure spirit
> . . . by an act of simple contemplation, in which there is no
> discursive succession of thought. The exterior and interior
> senses of the lower part of the soul cannot attain to this
> contemplation."
> (*Dark Night of the Soul*, Bk. 1, Ch. IX, No. 8). [9]

9 Translation: Kavanaugh, K., OCD, and Rodriguez, O., OCD, *op. cit.*, p. 315.

What St. John of the Cross so graphically describes is the experience of many sincere people who want to come close to God. It is like the Hound of Heaven — no matter what one does, no matter where one goes, the God of love tantalizingly follows. We know that our life is empty without him, but it is hard to find him — he seems deliberately aloof and hidden. What sort of prayer does St. John recommend for the person experiencing this night? He says that one should not try to meditate as one used to, but simply rest in the presence of God. He suggests a peaceful and loving attentiveness to God, waiting on him, patiently and with no anxiety. St. John goes so far as to say that this experience of the absence of God is "the night of contemplation," or that we pass from "knowing to loving."

St. John also describes this dark night as a kind of purgatory. To use another powerful metaphor, the Lord prunes the branches of the vine — and he does the pruning during the night. The Lord moves us on from one stage of the spiritual life to another, and he has to prune us of some of our past practices — practices which have, for the most part, been perfectly effective and praise-worthy. But God wants to reveal himself in another way which requires a very different prayer response. Our old ways of praying may have contained some elements of self-congratulations and self-confidence. The Lord wants to purge these away, and, in the doing, there may be quite an amount of suffering as the past consolations go, a greater self-knowledge comes to us and our Loved One seems hidden, indifferent and mysterious.

After some time we realize that this seeming absence of God is his way of showing himself to us in new and wonderful ways. We begin to get used to the darkness, and have to wait patiently on our Lord, because we are aware that the light is not far away. We learn not to rush our Loved One, but to wait, and do things his way and not ours. We need healing, reconciliation and liberating from so many of our past habits in order to move towards the Light of the dawning day.

St. John of the Cross presents us with a paradox. In this dark night it is not really dark, but we are just too blind to see. God is not really absent, he is closer than he has ever been, and we need our eyes to be healed. In one sense it may appear that we are doing nothing at the natural level of sense, intellect and feeling, the level at which we have always prayed. And in a sense we have to spend our time at prayer in doing nothing and wasting time patiently.

As well as a night of the senses, St. John speaks of a night of the spirit. Both nights are a contemplation infused by the Holy Spirit, working a purification in us. To describe more vividly what is happening to the person, St. John uses another metaphor — that of fire. He says the fire not only burns the wood on the outside, but begins to burn to the very center of the log, and the whole log becomes incandescent. And in the physics of St. John, the wood becomes fire in both *The Dark Night of the Soul*, and *The Living Flame of Love*. St. John expresses the process of the divinization of the soul effected by the penetration of the love of God or the Holy Spirit. It is a transformation which happens to the person, through no efforts of their own.

One of the greatest sufferings that people can experience as they advance into the depths of the dark night are their own sinfulness and unworthiness. At this stage of the dark journey we are tempted to despair and to give up the pilgrim way. We (to use a metaphor of St. John of the Cross) want to give up our ascent of Mount Carmel, because we find the going too tough. At this very stage, St. John says, we should not trust our own judgments but should keep on going. We need a good spiritual friend or counsellor who will recognize the stage of our pilgrim climb of the holy mountain.

At the very basis of this suffering is the difficulty in letting go, of not being in control, of really abandoning our lives to the

Lord. Our sinfulness and loneliness can be healed only by God
— and our role is to give God full freedom to work his divinization in our souls. All the ugliness we see in ourselves must be
surrendered to the Lord, and not be anguished over as if there
were something we could do about it, if only we could find the
correct solution. The person in this stage of the spiritual life
ought to simply hand everything over to the transforming love
of the beloved.

Marriage

One of the most sublime metaphors and symbols in the
whole of Christian spiritual literature is that of marriage. The
saints have struggled to describe the ultimate union between
God and the Christian, and many have used the analogy of a
bride and bridegroom, a lover and a beloved, a wedding feast. St.
John, in *The Living Flame of Love*, which marks the culmination
of his description of the spiritual life, speaks of mystical marriage. For St. John, the Lord is habitually asleep in the embrace
of the bride . . . "for if He be forever awake, communicating love
and knowledge, the person would already be living in glory." It is
certain that this is the ultimate goal of every Christian life, but
what is experienced in this life is a strong but obscure awareness
of the Lord asleep within the boat.

Both St. Teresa and St. John of the Cross say that we should
not be too concerned about this goal, but rather should work to
allow God to become the absolute Lord of our lives. This seems
to be the main point of the spiritual life, and of the teachings of
the Carmelite mystics — to allow the Lord love in our lives and
through us. Only those who are totally secure in this kind of
loving can live each day as it comes. It is freedom of the spirit
and a joy, celebration and liberation in the gifts that each person
has. When we move to this stage we experience a peace like the

first raptures of married love, filled with a new confidence, dark, mysterious and joyful.

Just like a newlywed, we have a new confidence of unquestioning trust in God, that he is our special lover, and will care for us and protect us whatever we have to do, or wherever we go. Our lives become more simple, like that of a trusting child, unquestioning the intentions of the loved one. This attitude is at the very heart of the spirituality of another Carmelite, Thérèse of Lisieux. Although she described it by using the metaphor of the child, it could be described as the unconditional love of the bride for the bridegroom and vice versa.

The spiritual life is like a marriage. There is the flush and excitement of bethrothal, the ecstasy of the honeymoon, and the working out of continually growing deeper in love. However, in the marriage ceremony both give their lives to each other "for richer for poorer, for better or for worse." We cannot love God if we have not learned how to love in our daily life — with our families and friends. Thus, a really good marriage is just as joyful and difficult as a spiritual relationship with God. This is why St. John of the Cross says when we learn how to love, we learn that even the deepest human love leaves us somehow incomplete. Often, as in a marriage, we learn the real meaning of love through the difficulties and dark spots.

For St. John of the Cross this marriage is with Jesus, an intimacy which is close to that of married couples, but far more intimate. In the beginning of the *Ascent of Mount Carmel*, he calls on the person to love Christ, and imitate him. In order to follow him closely we must study his life, get to know him and adopt his attitudes. With solid good sense St. John tells us that extraordinary experiences, visions, the miraculous, are not necessarily signs of the following of Jesus, but a simple commitment to the ordinary tasks and responsibilities of every day life. Just as a test of a good marriage is the ability to continue to love through the ordinary and the mundane, so St. John says the test of a healthy spiritual life is doing the ordinary things well for the love of Christ.

For St. John much of the life of coming closer to Jesus is a purgation of our old selves. We could today use a more up-to-date term: liberation. St. John of the Cross offers a spirituality of liberation for us today — he shows us how to liberate ourselves before we start liberating the Church or society. He seems to be saying that we need to be liberated before we can liberate. Thus, the practice of pastoral action, social education, political awareness — all of which have their own autonomy, are nevertheless united by a Christian concern that joins them together. St. John of the Cross offers an interior liberation, which helps us to be free for pastoral action and social concerns.

For reflection: individuals or groups

1. Who are the poets in your life? How much of a poet are you?

2. How much letting go have you had to do in your spiritual life? Has it caused you suffering and hurt? Would you describe it in terms of a "dark night"? How would you describe it?

3. How has your spiritual journey set you free? What have been the main elements of your inner liberation?

Hints for writing and sharing:

See the end of the introduction

References used in Chapter 5

Burrows, R., *Ascent to Love*. Dimension Books, Denville, NJ, 1987.

Centner, D., OCD., "Christian Freedom and the Nights of Saint John of the Cross," in Sullivan, J., OCD (Ed.) *Carmelite Studies* Vol. 2, ICS Publications, Washington, DC, 1982.

Green, T.H., SJ., *When the Well Runs Dry*. Ave Maria Press, Notre Dame, IN, 1979.

Sencourt, R., *Carmelite and Poet*. Hollis and Carter, London, 1943.

Smet, J., O.Carm., *The Carmelites Vol. II*. Carmelite Spiritual Center, Darien, IL, 1976.

Woodward, E., *Poets, Prophets and Pragmatists*. Collins Dove, Backburn, Vic., 1987.

_____ *Chapter 6* _____

St. Thérèse, Little Flower

The details of the life of St. Thérèse of Lisieux are fairly familiar to everyone, so we won't dwell on them. Suffice it to say that Thérèse Martin was born in 1873 and died Sr. Marie-Thérèse, a Carmelite nun in Normandy in 1897 at the age of 24. Her short life has amazed all who have read her autobiography and her biographies. She gained extraordinary insights into the meaning of life and enunciated an extremely simple formula for holiness. She drew on the spiritual heritage of Carmel, but added her own peculiar genius to the tradition. These can be summed up by the symbols and images Thérèse used in an attempt to describe her insights. The first is the Desert, the second is Mary's veil and mantle, the third is Spiritual Childhood/Little Way, and the fourth is Flower.

The Desert

Thérèse used quite frequently one of the great Carmelite symbols which we have not examined up till now — the Desert. The early Carmelites, and the Rule of St. Albert call the Carmelite continually back to the cell. There alone in the cell, the Carmelite seeks the Lord in the desert. Throughout the centuries, Carmelites have called their houses of special prayer, their hermitages, their houses of contemplation — deserts. For St. Thérèse, "Carmel was the desert where God wanted me to go and hide myself." In 1888 when she entered the convent for the first time, she said, "Everything thrilled me: I felt as though I was transported into a desert."

The experience of the desert for Thérèse is a freeing one, and an invitation to leave everything behind and set out on a journey of discovery. This would be a desert crossing — a separation from her familiar surroundings, into the austere environment of Carmel. The desert journey requires frugal meals, simple furnishings, humble surroundings, and a giving up of a protected middle-class lifestyle.

Like the Carmelites of old, Thérèse realized that when Carmel appears like a desert it is because there is no clear definition of what the future holds. When Moses crossed the desert with the Hebrews, they began to complain. They wished to return to the familiar and somewhat comfortable security of Egypt.

St. John of the Cross teaches that the desert allows us to reach the goal of finding God quickly. "The shortest way to the summit is through the desert of nothing." Thérèse wanted to go straight into the desert of solitude and silence, because she realized that she, the pilgrim, was walking towards the oasis at the center, and that oasis is God. The whole metaphor of the desert reveals for us a powerful insight into the spiritual life. We find as we journey in the desert that the Beloved does not stay in the oasis, because he moves out to meet us. It is our faith that teaches us that the Lord comes to meet us, and makes the journey with us.

Thérèse wrote from Carmel to her sister, Celine, "The wide open spaces, the magic horizons which open before you say profound things to your soul. I do not see any of those things, but I say with St. John of the Cross,

'In my Beloved I have the Mountains,
The lonely wooded valleys . . .
And that Beloved instructs my soul,
speaks to it in silence, in the darkness . . .

St. Thérèse tells us in her story that at times the night came during her journey in the desert. It appeared that she had not only lost her way, but had lost sight of the Lord. Most spiritual writers from the early Fathers until the present day say that this is the most profound experience of the desert; to come to the realization that the heart of the desert — is the desert of the heart. In the night of the desert journey, she no longer experienced the presence of Jesus and she is tempted to think he is absent. But she can say with the eyes of faith: "Blessed are those who have not seen, and yet have believed." She extended the metaphor by saying there was nothing to see but dry sand, but her faith convinced her that her journey would not end in a mirage.

For Thérèse her journey was with her Carmelite sisters, a small remnant of the pilgrim Church, just like the anawim of the Bible. They represented a communal experience which shaped her life and kept her in contact with the world and the Church. As a contemplative she echoed St. Teresa, that she was very much a daughter of the Church. Even in the desert she retained her vision of the world and her love went out to embrace all people.

On her desert journey the only guide she used were the Gospels. "It is especially the gospels," she wrote, "which sustain me during my hours of prayer, for in them I find what is necessary for my soul. I am constantly discovering in them new

1 Translation: Sheed, F.J., *The Collected Works of Saint Terese of Lisieux*, Sheed and Ward, London, 1949, p. 114.

lights, hidden and mysterious meanings." [2] To continue the image, she used the writings of the desert — those of St. John of the Cross which she devoured enthusiastically, and these guided her to that transforming love given to those who keep on the difficult desert journey.

The authenticity of her spiritual journey becomes apparent when we see that the more she loved Jesus, the more she loved her fellow travellers. Those who were her immediate sisters in the religious life were her constant concern, but her brothers and sisters in the world were those with whom she shared her joys and her sufferings. Whether they be convicts in prison, missionary priests in Vietnam, or relatives in Lisieux or Caen, she kept them all in her mind's eye. Her desert gave her huge horizons — a boundless perspective which gave her a spiritual responsibility for what she described as "millions of souls."

St. Thérèse and Our Lady of Mount Carmel

At various times some have suspected the "Carmeliteness" of St. Thérèse. [3] It has been said that she does not follow the spiritual paths set out by the "greats" of Carmel like St. Teresa and St. John of the Cross. Redemptus Valabek shows that in recent times, however, there is increasing evidence that Thérèse of Lisieux captured the essential traits of the Carmelite rationale like few other members of this religious family. The clearest pointer to her Carmelite roots is her tender and confident devotion to Mary, the Lady of Mount Carmel.

2 Translation: Clarke, J., OCD, *The Story of a Soul*, ICS Publications, Washington DC, 1975, p. 179.

3 See: Valabek, R., O.Carm., *Mary Mother of Carmel, Our Lady and the Saints of Carmel*, Vol. II, Carmel in the World Paperbacks, Rome, 1988, pp. 75-100.

In her famous statement: "Mary is more Mother than Queen" Thérèse shows how anchored she was in the earliest Carmelite understanding of Mary. Whereas at the time of the discalced reform, owing to cultural and political factors, Mary was often venerated as "Queen of Carmel," however, the more primitive appreciation of Mary was as mother. The fact that Thérèse did not make this statement for philosophical or theological reasons, but because this was her lived experience in Carmel, actually reinforces the conviction that Thérèse was a "natural" Carmelite.

As Thérèse was thoroughly Catholic, she had no restrictive concept of Carmelite tradition. In her devotional life she embraced all that she found worthwhile in the life of the Church. She chose all as a child; and in her later life she never changed. She had a great love of Our Lady, believing that Our Lady had cured her of a strange illness as a teenager.

Thérèse's charism was to grasp the inner dynamism of the commonplace ways in which God loved her. She would have been untrue to form had she not appreciated the central role of Our Lady in the Order of Carmel. The Order has no "founder" in the usual sense; through the centuries Carmelites have looked to Mary as the original inspiration of their way of life. Thérèse takes this for granted in a number of ways.

In a poem she wrote for her cousin, when she entered Carmel, she said:

"It is in the blessed order of the Virgin Mary
That I find genuine wealth." (*Poem 21*, 15 August 1895).[4]

From their very first chapel on Mount Carmel dedicated to Mary, Carmelites have been convinced that their family has the

---

4 Translation of the Poems: as quoted by Valabek, R., O.Carm., *op. cit.*

Virgin Mary as its mother. Thérèse expresses this traditional view:

"The Blessed Virgin is truly our mother because our monasteries are dedicated to her in a special way." (*Letter 154 to Leonie*, 27 December 1893).[5]

Thérèse believed that Mary led her to Carmel in the first place. "I love to think it is for this reason that she [Mary] was so kind as to make me her child ever more perfectly in granting me the great grace of leading me to Carmel" (*Letter 70 to Mother St. Placid*, December 1888, Vol. I, p. 482). Thérèse, who had become Mary's child on her first communion day when she had become a member of the sodality of Children of Mary, knows Mary as the sure guide who, even in a dark night, keeps pointing out the summit of Mount Carmel which is Christ himself. Towards the end of her life in dreadful sufferings Thérèse writes:

"O queen of the heavens, my beloved shepherdess;
Your invisible hand knows how to save me.
Even when I was playing on the rim of precipices,
You were showing me the very summit of Carmel.
I then must love if I am to fly to heaven."
(*Poem 53*, May 1897).

Much of the language of Thérèse sounds rather strange to our modern ears, but she shows she has the Carmelite fundamentals firmly in her life and grasp. She calls the scapular Mary's veil and mantle which reveals a basic understanding of the meaning of the scapular devotion: a symbol of dedication to

---

5 Translation of the Letters: Clarke, J., OCD, *St. Thérèse of Lisieux General Correspondence*, Vol. I and *Letters of St. Thérèse of Lisieux*, Vol. II, ICS Publications, Washington DC, 1982 and 1988.

Mary, and a sign of being associated with the life of the Carmelite family.

The Lisieux Carmel at this time earned some income by making and selling scapulars. Thérèse showed a deep understanding of the meaning of this Carmelite devotion when she wrote to a friend: "How happy I am that you are clothed with the holy scapular! Are you not united more closely still with your little sisters in Carmel?" (*Letter 166*). The scapular as a part of clothing symbolized the constant care that Mary had for her devotees. An ordinary part of a mother's care is to provide clothing for her children. In the spiritual life there are various ways in which this motherly charity of Our Lady is symbolized. Beyond the scapular Thérèse continually referred to the veil of Mary, under which her children were sheltered (*Poem 13*) or hidden (*Poem 1, 13*).

Far from being an escape, being hidden under the veil of Mary was important for Thérèse because it was under there that Jesus was to be found. "Jesus sleeps in peace under the folds of your veil" (*Poem 54:12*). And for Thérèse Jesus is everything (*Poem 45:5*). In this sense, for Thérèse Carmelite life was nothing else than remaining under the mantle of Our Lady. The white cloak of the Carmelite habit was a constant reminder of the mantle of Mary, which in medieval images covered the whole spectrum of the members of the Church.

In Carmel this cloak symbolized the purity of heart by which members of this religious family were to be characterized among all the followers of Jesus. Thérèse appreciated these truths even before she entered Carmel. She describes her experience at the shrine of Our Lady of Victories in Paris:

> "I understood that she was watching over me, that I was her
> *child*. I could no longer give her any other name but *mamma*,
> as this appeared ever so much more tender than mother.... I
> begged her about my dream to hide *beneath the shadow of her*

virginal mantle. When growing up, I understood that it was in Carmel I would truly find the Blessed Virgin's mantle and towards this fertile Mountain I directed my steps. I prayed to Our Lady of Victories to keep me far from everything that could tarnish my purity." (*The Story of a Soul,* trans. Clarke, p. 123).

For Thérèse, life in Carmel hardly had more basic purpose than to remain under Mary's protective mantle in order to present a pure heart reserved for the Lord. Mirroring the ancient Carmelite document, *The Institution of the First Monks,* Thérèse understood that Carmelites have as their charism: "the offering to God of a holy heart, purified of every actual stain of sin in a way that not only after death, but also in this life, they could to a certain extent taste in their hearts and experience in their minds the power of the divine presence and the pleasantness of heavenly glory" (*Institution of the First Monks,* in Analecta Ordinis Carmelitarum, [1914 to 1915] 348). Thérèse merely added the Marian dimension. To Celine she wrote . . . "hide yourself in her [Mary's] virginal mantle, that she will make you a virgin like her" (*Letter 105,* 10 May 1890, Vol. I, p. 618). As she recruits Celine to pray for the renegade Carmelite friar, Hyacinth Loyson, she feels responsible for this brother of Carmel, who for that reason is a son of Mary. "In any event, it is not our merits but those of our spouse, which is ours, that we offer to our Father who is in heaven, in order that our brother, a son of the Blessed Virgin, shall come back vanquished to throw himself beneath the cloak of the most merciful of mothers" (*Letter 129,* 8 July 1891, Vol. II, p. 729).

When she was dying Thérèse never ceased calling on Mary. A few hours before her death, the Prioress placed a picture of Our Lady of Mount Carmel before her and assured Thérèse that she would soon be caressing the Mother of Jesus. Mary had taught her well — there were no consolations in this final hour, nothing but purification, exile and suffering in the desert, journeying to Jesus.

Little Way

St. Thérèse's "little way" is not a childish conception of sanctity, but is really a very mature way of looking at the relationship with God. It is based on utter and complete confidence in God, an unconditional trust and love of God — this is the foundation of Thérèse's "little way" or doctrine of spiritual childhood.

Freud has shown how coping with one's parents can be an extremely liberating step to take. Many parents want to exert a deadening influence on even their grown-up children, and turn the beautiful notion of "family" into a false relationship. Many people are inordinately attached to their parents and their parents' world, and this can hold back the development of maturity. Marriages and progress in the religious life can be adversely affected by demands of parents and the guilt of children. The call of the desert, as Thérèse well knew is a call not to look back, but to be free from attachments so as to continue one's mature development in a relationship with God. Parents have to learn to "let go" and children have to learn to stand free and independent. This is a liberation, and a new sort of love develops between parents and grown-up children when this happens. Thérèse knew nothing about Sigmund Freud, but she realized that to travel across the desert of Carmel she had to trust not in herself or her own efforts, not in any created thing, but only in God. It took Thérèse nearly her whole life to discover her "little way."

Thérèse, in her dialogue with God, had become the listener rather than the speaker. She decided to trust simply in God. She describes how she had travelled through her life practically blind with stops, mistakes and hesitations along the way. She says that God showed her the "little way."

She grew to the realization that God loved her unconditionally simply because she was little, weak and powerless. She discovered God's love and mercy at the center of her whole life and she learnt that God's mercy is there for the little one precisely because she or he is a little one.

This insight was to give fresh meaning to her whole desert journey — the dynamic force of her life was confidence, knowing that whatever happened, wherever he led her, God's intervention was assuring and faithful.

As Conrad de Meester[6] explains Thérèse experienced a liberation when she meditated on the text: "Whoever is a LITTLE ONE, let him come to me!" (Pr 9:4). Thérèse felt herself personally called in this message God wanted to tell her something. She continued to search for the insights that the Lord would reveal to her about himself. She read Isaiah 66:12-13, "As one whom a mother caresses, so will I comfort you, you shall be carried at the breasts, and upon the knees they shall caress you."[7]

Thérèse explains in her own words: "Ah! Never did words more tender and more melodious come to give joy to my soul. The elevator which must raise me to Heaven is your arms, O Jesus!" For Thérèse the symbol of the elevator indicates that her way was a quick way to Jesus. She tells us that it is God who makes a person holy. "And for this I had no need to grow up, but rather to remain little and become this more and more. . . ."[8]

The condition for being among the "little ones" is to acknowledge that we are poor and needy and it is God who lifts us up. Thérèse teaches us the great lesson of the Carmelite school of mysticism: that in our seeming darkness and littleness

---

6 Conrad de Meester, OCD, *With Empty Hands*, St. Paul Publications, Homebush, NSW, 1982, pp. 46-58.
7 Trans. Clarke, J., OCD, *The Story of a Soul*, p. 208.
8 *Ibid.*, p. 202.

it is the light and strength of the Spirit which shows us how to proceed. She says we must entrust ourselves to God, and abandon ourselves. As Conrad de Meester notes, this is the very heart of Thérèse's teaching.

In St. Mark's Gospel when children were brought to Jesus, the disciples became annoyed. Jesus in his turn, was indignant and said to them: "Let the little children come to me, do not turn them away, for it is to such as these that the Kingdom of God belongs. I tell you solemnly, anyone who does not welcome the Kingdom of God like a little child will never enter it" (Mk 10:13-15.)

Fr. de Meester remarks that this was what Thérèse was thinking of when she said that she wanted to remain little, "to become this more and more," until she was just such a "little one." The abandonment of our own ways, the emptying of our heart permits the Lord to fill us with his gifts. We can now see that her little way is like the *nada* (nothing) of St. John of the Cross: her little way became the slogan of her life. She learned to allow God to be God in her life, to empty her hands and her heart and allow his mercy to take over.

Connected to the "little way" is Thérèse's use of the word mercy. While saying the divine office Thérèse would have often read this word in the psalms, but before the discovery of 1894, it did not appear to have awakened the same echo. Fr. de Meester shows that in all her writings previous to this date, and there are 300 pages of letters, poetry and plays, only once does the word appear and the adjective, merciful, one other time. After the discovery of God's mercy as the starting point from which the person who trusts in it becomes holy, we find the word, "mercy," used about 20 times in the first manuscript of her autobiography (about 200 printed pages). This is understandable because Thérèse was full of it, she was overwhelmed by the insights given her by the Holy Spirit.

So when, in January 1895, Thérèse began to write the

prologue of her autobiography, it was a meditative hymn of praise to this mercy of God, which she saw more clearly than ever before running like a golden thread through the fabric of her story.

The Flower

Thérèse realized that in the desert of Carmel were the springs of refreshment and life, and that is where the flowers bloomed. Thérèse saw herself as a flower, and this flower is her prayer. In trying to describe her prayer the best image is that of a completely trusting child talking to a loving parent. The best possible prayer is that of Jesus — the Our Father — a prayer of filial confidence. St. Thérèse pointed out that the highest degrees of contemplative prayer can be reached by a simple, loving recitation of the Lord's Prayer. Prayer is not a flower, but a weed, if it does not express our inner truth. Our lives, as well as our prayer, must be childlike in innocence, simplicity, truthfulness and ardor. Fr. Noel-Dermot O'Donoghue, a Carmelite friar,[9] writes:

> "Essentially the Christian way of Childhood is a way of entry into the Trinitarian mystery of fatherhood, filiation and that eternal breathing of love which is the Holy Spirit. The life and death of Jesus of Nazareth is the revelation of eternal childhood in history. The Eucharist is the most complete recapitulation now open to all that is, to God and men and all creation. It is a creative involvement in the dynamism of creation. It identifies with creation at the point where all creation is prayer, a response to the God who creates because he loves. It is not easy to achieve, because it demands detachment from the possessive self and from all that is finite and particular,

9 O'Donoghue, N.-D., OCD, "The Paradox of Prayer," *Doctrine and Life*, XXIV (Jan., 1974), pp. 36-37.

and it is never finally achieved. But it must be emphasized that the detachment is only the negative side; positively what is in question is a deep warmth and tenderness, an all-fathering, all-mothering love, for the child of God shares his father's attitude towards creation. It is in the child as beauty is in the flower; it is only in maturity that a human being can make his own of it, can detach the idea of it and make it a living ideal.

"As I see it, the basic dynamism of prayer, especially mystical prayer, is the affectivity of childhood, enlarged, refined and purified through experience. Experience presents us with much that is easy to accept, but it also presents us with the cross, and this is not easy to accept, certainly it is not easy to accept with open arms. Yet it is only insofar as we open our arms to the cross that we can open our arms to the world and that we can open our arms to God in filial love. It is the cross that extends our affection beyond the particular; in fact the very process of detachment from particular love is no small part of the experience of the cross. Mystical prayer is essentially the expression of a love that has grown beyond the particular by growing through the experience of the love of the particular, especially to particular persons. This love is full of pathos and loneliness, for it is an exile in the world; it is always being misunderstood in its most innocent and spontaneous expressions and manifestations, for the world can only understand love grossly, having lost childhood. It is deeply marked with the sign of the cross; otherwise it is not genuine. Yet if there is any state that may be termed blessed and heavenly it is here it is found, here and in the most perfect days of childhood.

"I think it must be admitted that the mystic will always be at odds with the world. There is nothing the worldly person, especially if he be a successful and respected clergyman, judges so quickly and so harshly as the mystical and the mystic, since he has by the very nature of his gift the simplicity of a child and leaves himself wide open to this judgment. Yet I do not despair that the world may change in this matter.

Rather, it seems to me, the world will have to change in this, or else one has to despair of the world. For today, for the first time in history man can destroy himself, and there is nothing more certain than that man will destroy himself utterly unless there is a change in the forces within him from which his decisions spring. The balance must shift from the perform- ance principle and all its attendant ambitions and hatreds in favor of the creative principle which has its final basis in the simple, spontaneous, as yet undifferentiated affectivity of the child. This is the way of mystical prayer. It is not a way of our own doing. It is the work of the Spirit of God. Our work is to prepare for his coming. Our prayer is that he may transform our prayer into the eternal love of the Son for the Father."

This quote from Fr. Noel-Dermot O'Donoghue, not only sums up the teaching of St. Thérèse of Lisieux, but expresses an important element in Carmelite spirituality. The spirituality of childlikeness, which is very strong in the Carmelite tradition, runs through much of the Christian spiritual heritage. It requires no strong personal acts, no glittering achievements, no spectacu- lar successes. It does demand total trust and love in God and a fidelity to the ordinary things of life.

This is Thérèse's teaching on prayer. Her basic attitude is one of simplicity in her lifestyle, her needs and expectations.

Thus, her prayer is not so much an I - Thou dialogue, but a Thou - I listening. She used the ordinary prayers like the Our Father, the Hail Mary, the Rosary to get started. She found the Gospels a helpful introduction to her meditations. She found inspiration for her prayer in the ordinary daily things, people, events and surprises. Some people ask to be taught to meditate or do contemplation, when they explain that they spend most of the day in the presence of God, and use frequent aspirations. These people are possibly closer to God than sophisticates in the methods of mystical prayer. Thérèse was one of these. So her flower of prayer was indeed a little one, but because of this, very pleasing to God.

For reflection: individuals and groups

1. Do you see your spiritual life in the simple terms that St. Thérèse uses like a "little way?" For you does she oversimplify the spiritual life?

2. How do you reach positively or negatively to the notion of spiritual childhood? Why?

3. What image or metaphor would you choose to describe your relationship with God? What insights does the use of your image give you to understanding your relationship with God?

Hints for writing and sharing:

See the end of the introduction

References used in Chapter 6

de Meester, C., OCD., With Empty Hands. St. Paul Publications, Homebush, NSW, 1982.

Hollings, M., Thérèse of Lisieux. Collins, London, 1982.

McNamara, W., OCD., Mystical Passion. Paulist Press, New York, 1977.

Valabek, R., O.Carm., Mary, Mother of Carmel, Vol. III. Carmel in the World, Paperbacks, Rome, 1988.

Blessed Titus Brandsma, Martyr

Blessed Titus was born Anno Brandsma on 23 February 1881 in Oegekloster in the Dutch province of Friesland. He came from a fervent Catholic family and one of six children, five of whom entered the religious life. At the age of 11 he went to the juniorate of the Franciscans, but was sent home owing to ill health. During the following years Anno gave serious consideration to his vocation, thinking he might join the Cistercians or the Carthusians. However, after taking advice he joined the Carmelites at the age of 17 in 1898, taking the name of Titus.

During his student days he showed a gift for writing and journalism by publishing his first book, which was an anthology of selected writings of St. Teresa of Avila. It was during these years he developed a great love for the spiritual heritage of the Carmelite order. By delving into the Carmelite writers of the past, he developed a lifelong habit of studying, writing about, and preaching on the spirituality of Carmel.

Blessed Titus was ordained a priest on 17 June, 1905 in the Cathedral of s'Hertogenbosch. He was sent by the Carmelite provincial to do post graduate studies at the College of St. Albert in Rome. Most of the time he spent in Rome he was sick, so, like

many northern Europeans, he did not develop a great love for
the Eternal City. He gained his doctorate from the Gregorian
University, and returned to Holland to teach the Carmelite
students in Oss. Whether he was busy teaching philosophy,
preparing a dogma course, proofreading an article for publica-
tion in a journal, he did everything in the spirit of Carmel — the
spirit of prayer and action.

He lived a prayerful but busy life, as teacher, retreat master,
writer, preacher and perpetual learner. Some of his activities of
these early years can be singled out — the Catholic University,
the Apostleship for the Reunion of Eastern Churches, and the
Catholic Journalists Association.

For years Blessed Titus had been sympathetic to the idea of
establishing a Catholic university in the Netherlands. Catholic
educators of the time sought his help. Together with the Dutch
bishops he did much to help found the Catholic University of
Nijmegen in 1923. With the university a reality Titus brought
about the foundation of the new Carmelite monastery in Nijmegen in 1929. Although the Nijmegen Carmel was to be his home
until shortly before his death in 1942, he was equally at home in
the nearby university where he lectured for 19 years. He was well
known for his enthusiasm for both Carmelite spirituality and
that of the Low Countries, as well as his great devotion to Mary,
the Mother and Sister of Carmelites.

His untiring efforts on behalf of the Catholic university
won him acclaim and he was appointed Rector of the university
in 1932. In his official capacity he became an even more familiar
figure on the Dutch scene. Among other duties, he went to
Rome to present Pope Pius XI with a report on the academic
standing of the university. Nor did Titus isolate himself in the
Netherlands, because he made several trips abroad; to Spain,
Germany, Ireland and the United States of America.

Shortly after his return from America in 1935, the world
saw Adolph Hitler's rise to power. Titus condemned the racist

philosophy of the Nazis in the monastery, the university and the pulpit. Dutch serenity was jolted in May 1940 when German troops invaded the Netherlands. The Dutch Catholic Church was strong, because Catholics formed nearly half the population, they owned a radio station, published daily and weekly newspapers, and had a well established system of Catholic schools. Once the invasion was complete, the Nazi propaganda machine went into action.

In 1941, the Nazis decreed that no priest or religious could be the principal or director of any school or university. Archbishop de Jong, the Archbishop of Utrecht, asked Titus to represent the bishops against the Nazis' attempt to undermine Catholic education. He travelled around the country encouraging Catholic communities to stand firm and keep the control of the schools in the hands of the Church. Next, the bishops asked him to present their case to the occupation administration in The Hague. After keeping him waiting for months, he was finally granted an appointment, but the quislings would not listen. His efforts on behalf of the bishops involved him in dangerous controversy between the Church and the Nazis.

The Church took on the invaders with a pastoral letter read in all churches in August, 1941 condemning Nazism. Catholics were told of the occupation forces' plan to disband Catholic orgnaizations, and especially to take over Catholic schools and the Catholic press.

The bishops realized that they would lose one of the most effective ways of communicating with their flocks if the Nazis either took over the newspapers or closed them down. Once again they asked the little Carmelite from Nijmegen to help them. Again Fr. Titus travelled the length and breadth of the Netherlands holding meetings and explaining to editors and journalists the stand the Church would take if the Nazis blocked their right to free press. The Nazis' Department of Information played their trump card by decreeing that it was illegal for any

Catholic newspaper to refuse to publish news or advertisements handed in by the National Socialist Party. Titus wrote a letter on behalf of the Dutch bishops to all the editors of Catholic papers, saying that the limit had been reached. As the spiritual director of the Catholic Journalists Association, he told the newspaper people that they had to stand firm and refuse to obey the Nazis. The last sentences of the letter were ominously prophetic:

> "We are not sure if those responsible will resort to violence. But in case they do, remember, God speaks the last word and He rewards His faithful servant."[1]

Blessed Titus made another tour of the country, but this time he visited all the bishops consulting them as regards the press. The Nazi propaganda headquarters sent articles to all Catholic papers with orders that they would have to print them. Archbishop de Jong answered with another letter referring to Titus' earlier letter, obliging the editors to abide by his instructions and refuse to publish lies and propaganda. Again, the archbishop asked the little friar to travel to all newspapers and this time he obtained written guarantees that they would stay loyal to the Church. All this resistance of the Nazis on behalf of the Church brought Titus to the attention of the Gestapo. He was arrested in January 1942 and on 26 July of that year he died in Dachau — one of the worst concentration camps built by the Nazis. During these months he showed himself, more than ever, as a person marked out for sainthood. Like another Carmelite, he wrote some of his most beautiful pieces in prison, his devotion to Mary grew stronger, and he began a life of St. Teresa of Avila, writing from memory. He showed so little concern for himself, but great compassion for his fellow prisoners, especially

---

1 Translation of quotes of Titus Brandsma: Valabek, R., O.Carm. (Ed.), *Essays on Titus Brandsma*, Carmel in the World Paperbacks, Rome, 1985.

in Dachau. When news of his death reached the Netherlands, Archbishop de Jong wrote to the Carmelites of Nijmegen:

> "He was a holy religious and holy priest, a man of great merit, possessed of great qualities, a founder of many works. He was always ready to assist me and I am greatly indebted to him. He gave his life for the Catholic Church."

Blessed Titus Brandsma more particularly gave his life for Catholic education and the freedom of the press.

Prophet

Titus Brandsma is a modern prophet of freedom of speech both inside and outside the Church. In Carmel, ministry comes from prayer and the love of God.

Zeal manifests itself first in prayer and asceticism, but also in the desire to be of service to people both in Church and society. Thus, it is understandable that both St. Teresa and St. Thérèse wanted to be men so that they could minister as priests. However, both stayed in their cloisters, and today we share in the fruit of their lives of love. Blessed Titus lived a life of prayer and action. On Carmel's coat of arms in the hand of Elijah is a flaming sword, and the motto reads: "I am consumed with zeal for the Lord God of hosts." Just as Elijah had to leave the solitude of Mount Carmel, to convert his people to Yahweh, so Blessed Titus had often to leave the monastery to bring God to people. He used to say that it was "leaving God for God."

This prophetic side of Titus' personality had a certain passion to it. Although he never gave up an opportunity to draw closer to God, and to strive after mysticism, his love of God drove him to an intense solidarity with the world. Within himself he possessed an interior resting place which was open to the world, but was anchored in God.

Like the prophet Elijah, Titus spoke out in defense of God and against evil in his time. Quite often he had to raise a critical voice in the Catholic Church of Holland. He frequently warned against the complacency of Dutch Catholics and attacked a comfortable "bourgeois spirituality" which he saw in the European Church. He attacked the practice, quite common in his time, by which Catholic schools retained teachers as temporary staff for years on end. This is a mark of an outspoken prophet who drew attention to injustice wherever he saw it. Even before the war he had condemned outright the unchristian materialism of Nazism. After the promulgation in Germany of the racist Nuremberg laws, he co-authored, "Dutch Protests against the Treatment of Jews in Germany" (Amsterdam, 1935). He wrote, "these acts against the Jews are deeds of cowardice. . . . To pretend that such behavior reveals the greatness of the Aryan race is pure madness; the madness of the weak." In 1939 he delivered a weekly lecture on Nazi ideology at Nijmegen University. He spoke about the fallacies of Nazi ideals at public meetings denouncing their persecution of the Jews — which provoked angry rebuttals in Nazi publications. Indeed, he was known only too well to the Council of Information for the Dutch Press, a Nazi front news service which he branded as a sewer. Before the invasion of Holland, Titus was a marked man.

Undaunted by the presence of the German army and their secret police, he continued to defend courageously the liberties of the people and the Church. In the spring of 1941, difficulties increased for the Catholic schools and the press. Blessed Titus became the champion of the Catholic cause. He moved around the country encouraging bishops, priests, religious and people to resist the Nazis as they tried to destroy the Church. He warned the press about Nazi censorship, describing it in colorful language: "a sewer of falsehood and imposture." To the journalists whose spiritual counsellor he was he said, "The day will come when The Hague will expect us to become the propagandists of Nazism. No, my friends, we must give way no further; there are limits, and we have reached them."

He wrote to the Catholic newspapers in the strongest terms:

> "The editors must categorically refuse those articles if they appreciate the Catholic character of their newspapers. It is not possible to act otherwise. We have reached the limit. I trust that Catholic newspapers will maintain the Catholic point of view without hesitation. The more we are united in refusing, the stronger we shall be."[2]

This act of prophecy cost him his life. Now the mild professor had become the dangerous little friar. The prophet was to become the martyr.

Titus Brandsma and Carmelite Spirituality

Blessed Titus Brandsma is a 20th century prophet to the Carmelite family, because he seems to describe the charism of the Order more clearly than anyone else. In an article published in the *Dictionnaire de Spiritualite* in 1936, he succinctly described the spirituality of the whole Carmelite family.[3] He began by stressing the antiquity of the Carmelite school of spirituality and explained that our great saints, St. Teresa and St. John of the Cross, had no other goal than to restore to the Order of Carmel

2 Valabek, *op. cit.*, pp. 53-54.
3 This summary of the famous article is based on the English translation from the French by Fr. Redemptus Valabek. It is found in Valabek, *op. cit.*, pp. 219-240.

its ancient spirit; they were not the founders of the Carmelite school of spirituality, but nevertheless are its restorers and its most brilliant lights. Their glory will not be diminished if the radiance which this school produced before their reform is shown. Far from being opposed to the first centuries of the Order, they often went there to seek examples. St. Teresa recommends the poverty of the early Fathers to her daughters; the memory of the hardships they endured in solitude should encourage Carmelites to bear theirs patiently, and the saint writes: ". . . All of us who wear this holy habit of Carmel are called to prayer and contemplation; this was our original institution, we belong to the race of those holy Fathers of Mount Carmel, who in such deep solitude and in complete renunciation of the world, sought the treasure, the precious pearl of which we speak."[4]

It was Teresa, in his opinion, who added psychological finesse to the primitive foundation of Carmel. The primitive and fundamental elements of the spirituality, he noted, from the beginning of the Order of Carmel are drawn from two sources — the imitation of Elijah and the veneration of the Blessed Virgin Mary. The Carmelites have always been mindful that they should imitate these two models, Elijah and Mary. They are the sons and daughters of Elijah and the brothers and sisters of Mary. From here also Carmel's mystical orientation proceeds.

He stressed that Carmelites have a special vocation to the mystical life. In *The Institution of the First Monks* the spiritual life of the hermits on Mount Carmel is described. It indicates clearly the double goal of the Order, and affirms consequently from the beginning its members' arrival at mystical graces if they are faithful to their rule and if God judges it opportune:

This life has a double goal; we acquire the first by our virtuous labor and effort with the help of divine grace. It consists in

4 Quoted in *Ibid.*, p. 219.

offering to God a holy heart, free of all stain of sin. We attain this end when we are perfect and in Carith, which is to say, hidden in charity. . . . The other goal of this life is communicated to us by a pure gift of God; I mean not only after death, but even in this mortal life, to taste in some way in one's heart and to experience in one's spirit the power of the divine presence and the sweetness of glory from on high. This is called drinking from the torrents of God's treasures (*Institution*, ch. 2).

Not only the purgative way and the illuminative way, but even the unitive way and infused contemplation are clearly proposed as the end to be attained, the goal to be pursued, the ideal to be realized; but this union and participation in the divine life are declared at the same time to be "a pure gift of God." Blessed Titus stated that never in any Order, to his knowledge, has a fundamental book or document called all its members so clearly to the mystical life.

He maintained that contemplation remains "the better part" for the Carmelites, and they have a special love of solitude. In his opinion the love of contemplation and the desire for solitude can be firmly attested from the documents of the medieval Carmelites, and the presence of hermitages and deserts can be seen throughout this period of Carmelite history. Indeed the necessity of poverty is given a different interpretation in Carmelite tradition from that of the Franciscans. For the Friars Minor poverty is an imitation of Christ and a rejection of the pomps of the world; for the Carmelite it is necessary to be poor when one tastes the pleasures of heaven in contemplation; the goods of this earth are nothing in comparison.

Blessed Titus claims that one of the constant elements of Carmelite spirituality is the practice of the presence of God. Inspired by the words of the Prophet Elijah, "The Lord lives in whose sight I stand," the *Institution* attaches special importance to the practice of the presence of God. This practice is a very efficacious means of living with God and meditating on his law "day and night," as the rule prescribes. In the medieval period there is evidence that Carmelites used the devotion to the Holy Face of Jesus as a way to practice the presence of God in their lives. Brother Laurence of the Resurrection and St. Thérèse of Lisieux are post-reformation examples of Carmelites who highlighted this element of the Carmelite tradition.

The Carmelites, Brandsma wrote, took a middle course between the intellectual and affective school of thought as regards contemplation. This is the emphasis of the medieval Carmelites, and finds faithful echoes in the synthesis of St. Teresa and St. John of the Cross. The western schism opened the door for mitigations, yet there remained those who were faithful to the tradition even to sanctity: St. Peter Thomas, who was one of the founders of the faculty of theology at Bologna, was a Frenchman from Perigard; St. Andrew Corsini in Italy; in Germany John of Hildersheim (1375), who in his *Historia Trium Regum* retains the traditions of the Order in remarkable fashion, and with him, representing the Carmelites of the school of Eckhart, Henry of Hanna; in England, the Carmelite translators of the works of Richard Rolle, the hermit of Hampole. Hermitages were established at this time in England as well as Italy, which proves that the ancient tradition was not completely forgotten.

Brandsma showed how there was a relationship of the Carmelite school to Ruysbroeck and the *Devotio Moderna* of the Low Countries. The affinity of Carmelite tradition to the *Devotio Moderna* is additional and significant indication of the middle and conciliatory position which the Carmelite school has taken between the different schools of thought on prayer and contemplation in the history of spirituality.

He showed how the Reform of Touraine was greatly inspired by the great reformer of the Order St. Teresa of Avila.

The reform of St. Teresa resulted in the separation of the reformed branch from the parent branch of the Order of Carmelites. But this result must be attributed to fortuitous circumstances and not to any formal opposition. What proves that the Old and New observances did not live in a spirit of opposition is the fact that shortly after the Teresian reform a very austere reform was introduced in France under the jurisdiction of the General. In the early years of the 17th century John Behourt and Philippe Thibault (d. 1638) started a stricter observance at Rennes in the Carmelite province of Touraine, of which a blind brother, John of St. Samson (d. 1636) was the soul and greatest mystical writer. There is no doubt that this reform was inspired by that of St. Teresa and reclaimed the ancient traditions. The writings of the members of the reform of Touraine, John of St. Samson, Daniel of the Virgin Mary, and Michael of St. Augustine give a clear exposition of the Carmelite traditions from the origin of the Order.

Blessed Titus Brandsma sees the Carmelite family in the metaphor of a tree having two main branches. He says that looking at Carmel from above, its two branches are united at their summits. He concludes his article in the *Dictionnaire*:

> Despite the separation which exists on the trunk, the two branches intermingle their foliage and blossoms without our being able to distinguish the one from the other. The blind singer of Rennes, John of St. Samson, does not have a different melody from that of the inspired singer imprisoned in the Carmel of Toledo, because both repeat what the Institution of the First Monks had inculcated in the Carmelites of the first centuries, namely that all Carmelites — Brothers and Sisters of the Order of Our Lady of Mount Carmel — in order to be faithful to their vocation should do their very utmost to go, under the guidance of the saintly hermit and prophet Elijah, across the desert of this life up to the Mount Horeb of the vision of God, strengthened by the heavenly nourishment which is shown on the altar.[5]

5 Quoted in: *Ibid.*, pp. 239-240.

Martyr

After his arrest, by the Gestapo on 19 January 1942 Blessed Titus was put in the state prison at Scheveningen where he underwent seven weeks of interrogation by his captors. When he was not being interrogated, he was in solitary confinement, which suited this lover of solitude. Here Titus wrote one of the most beautiful passages that he ever wrote, called *My Cell*. He propped his breviary open at the picture of Our Lady of Mount Carmel, and he mounted some holy pictures from his breviary: those of Fra Angelico's crucifixion, St. Teresa, St. John of the Cross with the motto, "To suffer and be condemned," and he also tacked onto the wall his favorite motto, "Take each day as it comes."

He began writing a biography of St. Teresa, but because he had used all his paper, he wrote it between the lines of his breviary. He was extremely peaceful and optimistic while he was in this prison cell. He wrote:

> Blessed solitude. I am quite at home in this small cell. I never get bored here — just the contrary. I am certainly alone but never was the Lord so near to me. I could shout for joy because now, when I cannot go to the people nor the people come to me, he reveals himself to me so often. Now he is my only refuge, and I feel so secure and happpy. If he ordered it, I would stay here forever. Seldom have I been so happy and content.

A few weeks after, Titus wrote his last poems *Before a Picture of Jesus in my Cell*:

> A new awareness of Thy Love
> Encompasses my heart:
> Sweet Jesus, I in Thee and Thou
> In me shall never part.

No grief shall fall my way but I
Shall see Thy grief-filled eyes;
The lonely way that Thou once walked
Has made me sorrow-wise.

All trouble is a white-lit joy
That lights my darkest day;
Thy love has turned to brightest light
This night-like way.

If I have Thee alone,
The hours will bless
With still, cold hands of love
My utter loneliness.

Stay with me, Jesus, only stay;
I shall not fear
If reaching out my hand,
I feel Thee near.[6]

After seven weeks at Scheveningen, he was taken to the concentration camp at Amersfoort. During the weeks of interrogation he fearlessly defended his condemnation of Nazism, and he wrote a summary of his views for them. He was called before the Nazi authorities who wanted him to sign a document saying that he would no longer preach or carry on his resistance to the occupiers of his homeland. He was told that if he signed there would be a good chance that he would be released, and that if he refused he would be sent to Dachau, and that meant certain death — a form of execution. After the war, the Gestapo file on Titus Brandsma was found and it revealed that they considered him as one of the most dangerous people in the Netherlands at that time. They wanted to get rid of him.

Consequently he was sent to Dachau where he survived

6 Quoted in: *Ibid.*, p. 30.

only five weeks. On 12 June 1942 he arrived at Dachau. He was stripped of his clothes, his head was shaved, and he was known as No. 30492. He now met specialists in brutality, where any manifestation of religion was forbidden and the fury of the guards was unbelievably cruel. Day by day his strength was leaving him.

At Dachau he had the Blessed Sacrament smuggled to him by a village priest. Blessed Titus administered the Eucharist to the prisoners by storing the hosts in his spectacle case. One day when he was carrying the sacrament, he was beaten by one of the guards who threw him to the ground and kicked him. He had to go to the infirmary, but he knew it was not so much a place of healing, as a laboratory of hideous experiments. While in the infirmary trying to recover from one of the beatings, he died on 26 July 1942.

The spirit of Titus Brandsma conquered the horrors of human degradation and cruelty. To the end he was intent on living out the Carmelite spirit, about which he had written so widely and so effectively. He refused to add to the hatred, cruelty and prejudice which he saw around him. This is why he shared his food with other prisoners, why he kept counselling, uplifting, consoling and forgiving. He even felt compassion for his executioners. Once when he had the Eucharist with him hidden in his glasses case, he woke in the middle of the night to pray to his Lord. He told this to a fellow Dutch Carmelite in Dachau. The Jesus he found in the midst of humiliation and inhumanity became his treasure and joy. When he was martyred, he was cremated like so many others of his fellow prisoners.

To be authentically the Church of the poor means to face rejection, misunderstanding, the determination to hamper her mission, violation of personal freedom, even to the point of murder and martyrdom. Martyrdom is the final accomplishment of life, and a free encounter with the Lord. What brought

Jesus to his death was a coherence between message and commitment. Gustavo Gutierrez sums up the act of martyrdom in these terms:

> "The testimony given by martyrdom shows clearly how ignoble are the maneuverings of the powerful, their accusations and their fears, and how far they are removed from the Gospel. The men and women who bear witness to their faith in the resurrection of the Lord are proof that those who sow death will depart empty-handed, and that only they who defend life have their hands filled with history." (G. Gutierrez. *A Theology of Liberation*, 15th anniversary edition, Orbis, Maryknoll, NY, 1988, pp. xliii-xliv).

Titus Brandsma is no plaster of Paris statue saint. He died because he was courageous and a plain speaking prophet, who spoke the truth. He will be remembered for his defense of human rights — freedom of the press, the right to education, and a just society for all. Titus will be remembered by Carmelites, in particular, because in word and deed he handed on the tradition faithfully, and, like his inspirers, Mary and Elijah, was prayerful and creative.

For reflection: individuals and groups

1. *Are there any modern martyrs whom you admire? What do you think motivated them, and gave them courage?*

2. *You may have mentioned prophets in an earlier chapter; have they had to face rejection, misunderstanding? How have they coped? How do you cope with rejection and misunderstanding in your life?*

3. *What is the inspiration in your life that helps you have the courage to make the decisions which you need to make?*

Hints for writing and sharing:

See the end of the introduction

References used in Chapter 7

Gluckert, L., O.Carm., *Titus Brandsma: Friar against Facism.* Carmelite Press, Darien, IL, 1985.

Valabek, R., O.Carm., (Ed.) *Essay on Titus Brandsma.* Carmel in the World Paperbacks, Rome, 1985.

Wijngaards, J., "A Saint from Holland" in *Tablet* (2 November, 1985), pp. 1151-1152.

_____ *C h a p t e r 8* _____

Blessed Edith Stein, Carmelite And Feminist

Her Life

Philosopher, educator, feminist, Jewess, Carmelite, martyr of the Holocaust — Edith Stein reveals that the Carmelite tradition in the 20th century has become very much involved in the tragedies and aspirations of the here and now. By her use of the imagery of the Cross in her life and writings she explains to us much about Carmelite spirituality.

Edith was born to Siegfried and Augusta Stein on October 12, 1891 in the city of Breslau in Silesia, now known as Wroclaw, Poland. She was the seventh surviving child in a middle class Jewish family and only twenty one months old when her father died. Her mother took charge of the family lumber business and raised her family as fervent Jews. They went to the local synagogue on the Jewish high holy days and they said prayers in their home every sabbath. In her autobiography, Edith says she was a headstrong child, she took to school enthusiastically and showed herself to be precocious for her age. At the age of seventeen she started at the Girl's High School in Breslau.

During her last years at the high school, the Stein family moved into a more spacious house called the "Villa" at 38

Michaelisstrasse, now called Nowowiejska. They were a very happy family not only with her mother, brothers and sisters, but with many loving uncles and aunts forming a close extended family. This closeness to her family and theirs for her was to form an integral part of her character and helped to determine her destiny.

At this time she said she lost the ability to pray and she called herself an atheist. In 1911 at the age of twenty she enrolled at the University of Breslau, in the Department of Experimental Psychology, a branch of the Philosophy Department. She wrote that between 1911 and 1913 the existence of the human soul was not acknowledged in the field of pyschology. She developed a lifelong love for art, music and literature — she wrote that attending a concert of Bach (whom she called her "Liebling," her "darling" or her "favorite") where Luther's hymn, "A Mighty Fortress is our God," was sung she was moved deeply by the third verse:

> Though hordes of devils fill the land
> All threatening to devour us
> We tremble not, unmoved we stand
> They cannot overpower us.

As she transferred from the University of Breslau to that of Göttingen, she was unable to believe in a personal God. However, she seemed to be called by the philosophy of Edmund Husserl, who taught in the Department of Philosophy. At Göttingen she came under the influence of some outstanding Jewish philosophers, Husserl, Adolf Reinach, Max Scheler and Theodor Conrad. She described the ancient university city:

> "Dear old Göttingen, I don't believe that anyone who did not study there between 1905 and 1914, during the short spring-time of the Göttingen phenomenology school, could ever imagine what that name conjures up for us."

Edith has given a description of the Göttingen Philosophy Circle, the star being Edmund Husserl born a Jew, but converted to Lutheranism when he was 27. When Edith sought admission to his classes, he asked if she had read any of his works, and when she replied that she read the whole of the second volume of his *Logical Investigations*, he thought this to be an heroic feat and readily admitted her.

Husserl had established the new discipline of *phenomenology*,[1] which proved an exciting new world for Edith. It as an entry into a religious as well as philosophical atmosphere because the leaders of the Göttingen circle were men and women of deep spirituality. Many of Edith's confreres at the university were Jewish, and there was an affinity between the Jewish radical nature and the emerging phenomenological philosophy.

Husserl recognized his debt to the great Catholic medieval theologian and philosopher, St. Thomas Aquinas, saying that phenomenology converges towards Thomism and prolongs it. With Husserl, ontology[2] was now given new respect because he recognized the reality of the visible objective world, but also the need to postulate the reality of a transcendent one. This was not a very popular approach in the European universities of this time.

Edith considered herself to be an atheist. When she came to the University of Göttingen, she saw that the leading intellectuals there were studying the structure and meaning of deep universal truths which they regarded as being just as real as any other phenomena. They discussed their new philosophical

---

1 Phenomenology is used by Edmund Husserl, Edith Stein's philosophical mentor, in a special sense. The goal of phenomenology is to clarify and thereby to find the ultimate basis of all knowledge.

2 Ontology is a branch of philosophy which looks at the very essence of things. Another term allied with this is metaphysics.

perspective as a search for the sacredness of being and the purity of the reality of the basis of all things.

Edith's atheism was confronted by these philosophers who wanted to understand the very mystery and key to all existence. The Jewish and Christian notion of Revelation, then, became a valid object of their investigations. Under the influence of Husserl, she studied the Greek philosophers and the medieval Scholastics. She was also impressed by the spirituality of two other professors, Max Scheler and Adolf Reinach. Scheler was a Jew who had converted to Catholicism, and Edith writes that he had more profound influence on the students than Husserl.

As she came to the end of her stay at the university she presented her doctoral thesis entitled *On the Problem of Empathy*[3] in which she studied the "psycho-physical individual." This topic became the main theme of all her life's writings. She wanted to look at the responsibility that one has as a member of the human family. She analyzed the individual as the "I" of the "self," but also wanted to see what is the relationship to the "other." This proved to be a lifelong search and became part of her life and character as a woman who had a very deep sense of her belonging to a human family, with all its destiny, with its hopes and aspirations. She actually lived what she was studying in the halls of philosophy — this can be seen throughout her life — in her deep concern for her own family, her becoming a nurse during the First World War, her care for her friends and pupils, her solidarity with the plight of the Jews in Nazi Germany, and her concern for her Carmelite sisters.

In 1915 Edith became a Red Cross nurse and served for six months in Moravia nursing Austrian soldiers infected with dysentery, cholera and spotted fever. In 1916 she received her doctorate "summa cum laude," and was invited by Husserl to be

3 Stein, Edith, *On the Problem of Emphathy*, Trans. Waltraut Stein. *The Collected Works of Edith Stein*, Vol. 3, ICS Publications, Washington DC, 1989.

his first assistant at his new post at the University of Freiburg. This was most unusual in the Germany of that time to have a woman in such a position.

She left this post in 1918 and returned to her family home in Breslau. From this time until 1921 was a period of intense struggle in her life, because she was considering becoming a Christian. She knew that such a step would bring untold sadness and suffering to the members of her loving family, but she also knew that she would never have any interior peace unless she followed the calling of God.

Edith decided to enter the Catholic Church in 1921 after reading the autobiography of St. Teresa of Avila. On January 1, 1922, at the age of thirty, she was baptized in the church of St. Martin in Bergzabern. After her baptism, Edith retired from university circles and took a teaching job for eight years at the Dominican Sisters school of St. Magdelene's in Speyer. She taught high school girls, novices and nuns preparing for a teaching career.

During the years 1922 through 1933, Edith taught, wrote, studied, gave lectures, attended conferences, pursued her scholarly life as a well known philosopher and developed her spiritual life as a Catholic. At Speyer she lived a very simple lifestyle, saying the divine office each day, keeping three private vows of poverty, chastity and obedience, and she accepted very little reimbursement from the nuns for her services. At this time her colleagues and pupils described her as a loving, humble, modest and patient person, who always seemed very peaceful, balanced and serene.

During these years she not only developed into a renowned philosopher, but she became a European leader on the place of women in the world. She delivered many lectures on women's issues, and she was closely allied to the League for Catholic Women and the Association of Catholic Women Teachers.

As the dark of Nazism gathered in Germany, Edith was

considering entering the Carmelites. In her essay *The Road to Carmel* she links the coming persecution of her people, the Jews, to her entrance into Carmel. She writes:

> "I spoke to our Savior and told him that I knew that it was his cross which was now being laid on the Jewish people. Most of them did not understand it; but those who did understand must accept it willingly in the name of all."[4]

When she made her decision to enter Carmel, she believed that the Carmelite order permits her sons and daughters to freely and joyfully participate in the drama of Christ's redemptive work. She wanted to participate in such a way that she could spend the rest of her life praying for the Jews and making reparation for the horrors of the Nazis.

Her decision to join religious life as a contemplative Carmelite nun caused her family much anguish and sorrow. If her conversion to Catholicism had been painful for them, her entering Carmel was inconceivable, and on the eve of their persecution seemed unbelievable. One member of this close family wrote: "A cleft existed between her and her family which could not be reconciled although, on the other hand, we could not stop loving her."

On October 14, 1933, at the age of 42 she joined the Carmel of Cologne on the eve of the feast of St. Teresa of Avila, who, in a sense, had lead her home. She took the name of Sister Teresa Benedict of the Cross, reminding herself of her debt to Teresa of Avila, to John of the Cross and to the spirit of St. Benedict coming to her through her close association with the Benedictine Abbey of Beuron. All who saw her at this time remarked that she was very happy and joyful, and she reports

4 Quoted in Oben, Freda Mary, *Edith Stein, Scholar Feminist, Saint*, Alba House, New York, 1988, pp. 26-27.

that she hadn't laughed so much in all her life as during the two years of her novitiate.

She continued to feel a close affinity with the Jewish people as their persecution intensified and the German expansion began to spread throughout Europe — in 1936 Hitler took the Rhineland, 1938 Austria and later that year Czechoslovakia. During 1936 Edith experienced both great sadness and happiness when her mother died and her sister Rosa asked for baptism and wanted to live at the Cologne Carmel. It was decided that it had become too dangerous for Edith in Cologne and she moved to the Carmel of Echt in Holland. In 1940 Rosa came to Echt to act as portress for the Carmelite nuns, but it became very difficult for both Edith and Rosa because the Nazis invaded Holland in May of that year.

On July 1, 1942 the education of Catholic children of Jewish descent in Catholic schools was forbidden by the Nazis in Holland. This lead to a protest by the Dutch bishops as well as several protests about the deportation of Jews from the country. As we have seen these protests lead to the death of Titus Brandsma, and it also lead to the death of Edith Stein. In retaliation the Nazis ordered the deportation of all Catholics of Jewish descent. The Gestapo came to the Carmel and took both Edith and Rosa.

They were taken to three camps — Amersfoort, Westerbork in Holland and finally to Auschwitz. In the transport of 559 people from Holland were two Jewish sisters, Edith and Rosa Stein. The deportees were ordered to form lines of five. The SS doctor selected 295 persons he considered fit for work, while the others, 264 including Edith and Rosa, were driven in trucks to huts in the woods where they were told they would shower and be deloused.

Edith had to take off her Carmelite habit, Rosa her secular clothes, and naked they were herded into the death chambers and murdered by Zyklon B poison gas. Their bodies were thrown into mass graves, but towards the end of that year their bodies were burned. Edith Stein was martyred on August 9, 1942.

Edith Stein — Feminist

Of the many contributions that Blessed Edith made to the world — her philosophy, theology, spirituality, ethics — her contributions to the debate on the position of women in the world and the Church is timely. She wrote on this question some forty or fifty years before this debate came to general attention of the public in western countries in the 70's and 80's of this century.

As a teacher of philosophy in a university and later as a teacher of girls in a high school, she was concerned about the appropriate education of women in modern society. In order to speak on questions of education, she studied an analysis of woman's nature and place in the world. In a lecture on this topic in 1928, she challenged the masculine bias of the European education system and commented on the unique value of the feminine psyche.

In her *Essays on Woman*[5] Edith produced an ontology of woman — an explanation of her nature, being and her destiny. She believed that human beings — men and women — are equal and complementary. "There is no question (in the biblical account) of a *sovereignty* of man over woman. She is called his *companion* and *helpmate*, and a man is told that he will cleave to her and that they will become one flesh."[6]

---

5 Stein, Edith, *Essays on Women*, Trans. Freda Mary Oben. *The Collected Works of Edith Stein*,
   Vol. 2, ICS Publications, Washington DC, 1987.
6 Stein, Edith, *ibid.*, p. 60 (the italics are the author's)

She held that as long as there is a respect for marriage, the family and the care of children, women should engage in professional activities outside the home. She believed that there is no area of professional life that women could not fulfil.

She wrote that Catholic thought must meet the challenging questions of this century: women's vocation, sexual problems, teaching on marriage and so on. In spite of the high regard that Jesus had for women during his ministry and the important role they played in the life of the early Church;

> "In the course of time women were eliminated from all ecclesiastical offices. Their status in Church law gradually worsened. In most recent times we have witnessed a change, owing to the powerful demand for women helpers in charitable and parish work. There is a desire among women that these activities should once more be given the character of a sacred ecclesiastical order, and it is quite possible that one day this wish may be conceded."[7]

It seems that Edith did not advocate women priests, but these forceful words are remarkable when we realize that they were written about 1930.

She encouraged women to become involved in the social, political and economic issues of their time. For Edith the most pressing issue of her time was the propagation of German Nazism with its horrific racism, militarism and authoritarianism. She saw the Hitler philosophy as fundamentally opposing the dignity of every human person — dignity and respect for each human person was the very basis of all her beliefs and writings as a philosopher and teacher, and later as a Carmelite

---

7 Phelim, Fr., OCD, *Edith Stein in her Writings*, Carmelite Publications, Loughrea, Ireland, (No date provided).

theologian. The Nazi's disregard for the human person led to their persecution of the Jews, their demeaning of the position of women, and their readiness to crush all opposition.

Once Edith had described the ontology of woman, she proposed Mary, the Mother of Jesus, as the model for women. She rejected the portrayal of Mary in many popular devotions of the Catholic Church and in the Marian poetry of popular hymns. On the contrary, she put forward to modern women, Mary, the woman standing at the foot of the Cross of Jesus, uniting both tenderness and power. She believed that the caring maternal force of women is necessary for both the world and the Church. For her, the greatest title for Mary is that of Mother — very much in line with the Carmelite tradition's view of Mary. She considered that all women, like Mary, are called to exercise that maternal mystique whether they be married, single or in the religious life.

Edith Stein also developed a theology and a philosophy of education for women. When scholars extract from the corpus of her works her educational theories, she will take her place with the great educationists like Maria Montessori, John Dewey and Paolo Friere. It will be for Carmelites and others to use her timely theories on the education of women to remove the many injustices which women still experience in many parts of the world. She wanted girls to receive that kind of education that will open their life to the transforming love of God, to become maternal either physically or spiritually, and to use their tenderness and power in the home, the Church and the world.

Edith Stein's feminism underlines that line of thought running through the Carmelite tradition — the necessary balance of the masculine and the feminine aspects of Carmelite life.

Edith Stein and the Cross

Our understanding of the mystery of evil in the world and in our lives has always been a problem for men and women. Edith Stein's use of the imagery of the Cross helps us to understand the horror of the Holocaust and her martyrdom. For her the Cross meant much more than bearing our suffering and carrying our burden in life — for her it meant faithfulness, hope and love. In fact, this is her secret, this is the secret of understanding her life.

Edith showed her faithfulness to God just as Jesus had shown his fidelity by following the Father's will even if it led to his crucifixion. Edith remained faithful to God's calling even when it separated her in sorrow from her family, and led to her humiliating murder. She emptied herself and surrendered herself to God, and thus remained free and powerful and was not conquered by evil, but triumphed, not only over Hitler, but over evil itself. Until the very last moment of her life she remained free and powerful, which can only be achieved by that faithfulness to God and the Cross.

The Cross, for Edith, meant hope as opposed to despair. She maintained that her hope and trust in God would bring about the triumph of good over evil. She believed that in spite of the tragedy of the Holocaust, God would bring about peace. At her beatification in Cologne on 1 May 1987 Pope John Paul said, "She saw the inexorable approach of the Cross. She did not flee in fear. Instead she approached it in Christian hope with love and sacrifice and in the mystery of Easter even welcomed it with the salutation 'Ave crux, spes unica' (Hail cross, our only hope)."[8]

---

8 Quoted in Stein, Waltraut, J.H., "Reflections on Edith Stein's Secret" in *Spiritual Life*, Vol. 34, No. 3 (1988), p. 133.

The Cross meant love. God had shown his uncompromising love for us by becoming a human person in absolute solidarity with us. Throughout her life Edith Stein imitated in so many ways this uncompromising love and solidarity for her fellow human beings. She became a nurse in the First World War, she had a deep commitment to her family and to her fellow Jews, she spent her Carmelite life in prayer and writing — a commitment of love for all people. The Cross gave her an understanding of the power of prayer, and of surrender to God which overcomes the turning away from God in evil.

She wrote:

"And God can, for love of a soul which he has taken up for himself, draw another person to Himself. That the divine freedom submits himself to the wishes of his chosen ones at the time that he listens to prayer is one of the marvelous facts of the religious life. Why this is so goes beyond all comprehension."[9]

Edith believed that her life of loving surrender to God and solidarity in prayer gave her the power of freedom and peace. Thus her martyrdom cannot be explained as desire to die, or of being a nobody, or of a sense of guilt. No, her martyrdom is a victory coming from her understanding of the symbol of the Cross of Jesus. Her martyrdom comes from her sense of the fullness of being a person who in the eyes of God was loved and cherished, from her sense of inner peace, and from her love.

Her last work as a Carmelite theologian was her *Science of the Cross*.[10] In this book she meditated on the writings of St.

---

9 Quoted in Oben, Freda Mary, *op. cit.*, pp. 67-68.
10 Stein, Edith, *The Science of the Cross: A Study of St. John of the Cross*, Eds. Lucy Gelbert and Romaeus Leuven, OCD, Trans. Hilda Graef, Henry Regnery, Chicago, IL, 1960.

John of the Cross, the great Carmelite mystic who helped Edith to fathom the depths of our relationship with God. Her upbringing in a loving Jewish family, her education as a philosopher, her living of the Carmelite life — all culminated in her understanding of the Cross and her martyrdom.

It may appear that her death and the death of the millions who died with her in the Nazi gas huts was pointless. But the recognition of her sacrifice is symbolic of the solidarity between Jews and Christians. Beyond the evil, the horror, the cruelty is something far more powerful. It is love which binds us all together in love and in the all-encompassing love of God. It is not simply a matter of forgive and forget. Edith Stein's martyrdom means that reconciliation comes by remembering the possibility of evil, by learning that love transcends evil and that it is possible to live in peace.

Her feastday is celebrated on 9 August, the anniversary of her death at Auschwitz.

For reflection: individuals and groups

1. *Edith Stein had the experience of all martyrs: when they are in the hands of evil persons they appear extremely weak and powerless, but, in fact, they are at the stage of their most powerful and strongest. How do you feel at times of powerlessness and weakness? Does your faith in God help you to be strong and powerful? What does strength and power mean to you?*

2. *Blessed Edith spoke about a total surrender to God. How do you totally surrender yourself to God? Do you try to avoid this concept and challenge? How does a total surrender to God affect your life? Edith Stein said that a total surrender to God gave her freedom and love. How do you explain this? Do you have a similar experience?*

3. *For Edith, most of her life was summed up in the Cross. How do you experience the Cross in your life? By accepting the Cross or the crosses in your life, do you also experience the Resurrection? How can the Cross and Resurrection go together?*

Hints for writing and sharing:

See the end of the introduction

References used in Chapter 8

Bassehart, Mary Catherine, "Edith Stein's Philosophy of Person" in *Carmelite Studies*, Vol. IV, ICS Publications, Washington DC, 1987, pp. 34-49.

Oben, Freda Mary, *Edith Stein, Scholar-Feminist-Saint*. Alba House, New York, 1988.

Oben, Freda Mary, "Edith Stein the Woman" in *Carmelite Studies* Vol. IV. ICS Publications, Washington DC, 1987, pp. 3-33.

Stein, Edith, *Life in a Jewish Family 1891-1916: An Autobiography.* Trans. Josephine Koeppel, OCD. The Collected Works of Edith Stein, Vol. 1, ICS Publications, Washington DC, 1986.

Stein, Edith, *Essays on Woman.* Trans. Freda Mary Oben. The Collected Works of Edith Stein, Vol. 2, ICS Publications, Washington DC, 1987.

Stein, Edith, *On the Problem of Empathy.* Trans. Waltraut Stein. The Collected Works of Edith Stein, Vol. 3, ICS Publications, Washington DC, 1989.

Stein, Waltraut, H.H., "Reflections on Edith Stein's Secret" in *Spiritual Life*, Vol. 34, No. 3 (1988), pp. 131-135.

_____ *Chapter 9* _____

Carmelite Spirituality Today

One of the most helpful themes of present day spirituality is the following in the footsteps of Jesus under the guidance of the Holy Spirit. This has led to a stress on the humanness of Jesus, the Jesus of history and the Christ of faith as found in the Gospels. This contemplation of Jesus has become the model for Christian living in the contemporary Church. This has freed us from a tendency to encourage an angelic spirituality, and a flight from the world and created things. Devotion to the Jesus of the Gospels has given the Church a more solid Christology and a spiritual foundation for the ministry in the Church and the world.

This contemporary thrust has challenged the Church to become the welcoming community, the pilgrim people of God, the Church of the poor, and the sacrament of the suffering Christ. This is a somewhat more humble description of the followers of Jesus, than was the description of the Church as triumphant. The Jesus of the Gospels shows us how he carried out his mission confronted by the challenges of his time. The humanness of Jesus is even more vivid for a people who are searching for the new face of Christ, who is the response to their legitimate aspirations for justice and freedom.

This attitude towards Jesus finds echoes and support in

Carmelite spirituality. The Rule of St. Albert calls us "to live in the footsteps of Jesus Christ, and serve him faithfully with an uncluttered heart and open mind." The rule goes on to say that Christ is present to us throughout the day, especially in the continuous contact with the Word of God. This Christocentric perspective of the rule implies the rediscovery of Gospel radicalism, and the following of the Gospel values in simplicity.

Carmelites see Mary as a perfect model in the following of Christ. She welcomed the Word of God, and Jesus was the very reason for her existence. Mary knew how to listen to God, to contemplate his message, and to show us how to come close to Jesus. She is the perfect image of the disciple of Christ, having lived out in her life all the attitudes and values proclaimed by Christ. Because she treasured all these things in her heart, she is the model of contemplative prayer in the Carmelite tradition. We look on Mary to understand and live her way of listening to and answering the Word of God. Mary leads us to a threefold openness: 1) open to God through prayer; 2) open to ourselves through an understanding of our own identity; 3) open to others through service, especially to the poor and the alienated.

The spirit, the personality, and the work of Elijah dominate the sacred site of Mount Carmel. In his prayer and reflection the great prophet heard the call of God to bring his people back to him. With ardent zeal, prophetic courage, and a certain amount of passion he answered the call of God. The prophet is so present to God that God dominates his whole life. He is moved by the needs of the people who are being neglected and being misled. Our times could be described a bit like those of the prophet Elijah, because we live in times of profound social upheaval, changes in the Church, and times of injustices which render people slaves to false gods. For this reason, Carmelites see Elijah as a model of one who hears the Word and does it. The prophet is the one who "allows God to be God in our time." In this way Carmelite spirituality encourages people to live continually in the presence of God, and like the prophet to be attentive to the signs of the times, so that they may hear the cry of the poor.

Like the great inspirers of Carmel, St. Teresa had a great devotion to what she called the humanity of Christ, especially his sufferings. She said that her sustenence in prayer was the Gospels, and it was practically the only book she used. Her love of Jesus and her following of him was central to her life. It was because of Jesus she was moved to live a life of radical poverty, fraternal love, and singleness of heart. In an effort to come closer to Jesus she wanted to bring Carmel back to the utter simplicity of the life of the first brothers on Mount Carmel. In today's world, St. Teresa speaks to us again as we try to follow Jesus in the poor, the oppressed and the neglected ones of our society.

St. Teresa's devotion to the passion of Jesus reminds us of the total commitment of Jesus, reaching the extreme limit of martyrdom. It is here that the love of Jesus is itself both radical and full of hope for those who are the oppressed of this world. The persecution, the sufferings, and the martyrdom of Jesus will always be the most radical model of Christian commitment, and the cost of discipleship. Thus meditation on the lifelong fidelity, the rejection, and the death of Jesus leads us to the hope of the resurrection.

St. John of the Cross reminds us that to imitate Jesus we must continually study his life. John does not put much importance on mystical experiences, because they are not completely centered on the imitation of Christ, the abandonment of our selfishness, and the service of those in need. For St. John, the graces of prayer and the spiritual life have no value in themselves, they must lead to self-surrender for others.

St. Thérèse wanted to find Jesus in the desert and was prepared to follow him wherever he led her. Her way was one of complete trust in him. Her humility allowed Jesus to cover up her weaknesses and imperfections. Blessed Titus and Blessed Edith followed Jesus as academics and prophets, which led to their martyrdom.

Thus, in the post-Vatican II renewal of Carmel there has been a call to follow Jesus as the Jesus of the Gospels, the Jesus who challenges the misuse of religious and secular power, the Jesus who has a special option for those who are not getting a fair go in this world, those whom society would prefer to forget.

Tension between Contemplation and Action in the Carmelite Tradition

Throughout the centuries there has been a tension in the Carmelite tradition between contemplation and the active apostolate. We see this in the Rule of St. Albert, the writings of Nicholas the Frenchman, and the Institution of the First Monks. Fundamentally Carmelites are called to the contemplative life, but what this meant in practice has exercised the hearts and minds of many Carmelites.

Blessed Titus Brandsma explained the tension in terms of the "mixed life." He said that the Dominican tradition says that one contemplates the Word of God and then goes out and hands on the fruits of the contemplation to others by preaching and teaching. However, the Carmelite tradition is different. Blessed Titus explains that the Carmelite is called to a life of contemplation which is continual and all-embracing and can be interrupted only by the needs of the apostolate — he used to say quite often that the Carmelite is called "to leave God for God." This means that when God calls Carmelites to the apostolate they move from one mode of encountering God to another, but they prefer the contemplative mode.

However, today Carmelites reflecting on their contemplative tradition, can offer to Christians a synthesis in the secularized world in which they find themselves. Like the Carmelite tradition, many say that all Christians are called to contemplation and mysticism. For example, Karl Rahner says that all

Christians in the Church of the future must be mystics, Gustavo Gutierrez says that all the baptized are called to contemplative prayer, and Segundo Galilea says that all the baptized are called to contemplation and commitment. How can these theologians say this? What do they mean?

The focus for the answer is on the notion of contemplation in the Bible.[1] Segundo Galilea writes that in the biblical tradition there has been a synthesis between contemplation and commitment. The theme of contemplation in relation to liberation and its demands of commitment appears of prime importance. The synthesis of the active apostle and the contemplative in the Church of today is urgent. This is so much more necessary now because of the misunderstanding created during the recent past by various "types of spirituality" among Christians. Sometimes contemplation is seen as a flight from the responsibilities of this world and the concern for one's brothers and sisters. This understanding came from a platonic dualism which stressed the individualistic, the transcendental and a separation from the concern of the world.

However, alongside this influence has been a biblical interpretation of contemplation which is far more relevant for Christians in today's Church. This can be seen, for example, in the witness of the prophets, especially Elijah. They are guides of the people, critics of a system, proclaimers of a message of liberation, which arises from their contemplation of the Word of God, which impels them to action. This is the mystical tradition which springs from the people and from the Word and not from power.

In this contemplative tradition we must situate the figure of Elijah as a symbol and archetype. It is typical of mystics in action that they have had a very deep experience of God in the desert,

---

1 The following section pp. 138-149 has been inspired by S. Galilea. *Following Jesus*, Orbis, Maryknoll, NY, 1981, Chs. V and VI.

and without ceasing to be influenced by this experience he showed the people the true religion and freedom from oppression. Service in the liberation of people through their participation in prayer and community activity is very likely to be the definition of the Christian in the secularized world of today.

In this enterprise the contemplative quality of Elijah led him to come face to face with the absoluteness of "the other" in the solitude of the desert and Karith. This was together with the absoluteness of "the others" in whom his experienced faith led him to discover a people among whom God dwells, and to whom he had to announce the freedom of the children of God. This contemplative quality also allowed Elijah, the mystic, not to be discouraged by this people who often showed themselves as fickle and mediocre. Thus, he had to be content and patient in the loneliness of his prophetic leadership. In this prophetic solitude, Elijah remained firm in hope.

This hope which belongs to what some call "political prophecy," sustained Elijah even when his mission seemed hopeless. He sacrificed power to help in the liberation of his people, faithful to his contemplative grace.

Segundo Galilea points out that the biblical case of Jesus is equally enlightening. His contemplation leads to a commitment. It had socio-political consequences related rather to evangelization than to political action. Jesus offers a liberation which is far more encompassing — an inner liberation from our doubts, our fears, our weaknesses, and our sinfulness, as well as liberation from the oppression of the unjust structures which imprison us. This is the ultimate form of liberation described for us in the Bible, and finds its ultimate symbol and archetype in the life and message of Jesus.

Fr. Galilea says that the commitment of the contemplative to others can be seen under two aspects. The first is a political option. Here Christians serve Christ in the service of others by encouraging political and social development; and to do this they must participate in political power. Here their commitment becomes more partisan politics.

The second way of commitment to others is that of the prophetic option. Here charity, the source of contemplative prayer, is directed towards the proclamation of Christ's message about the liberation of the poor. This message leads to our forming a critical consciousness and enhances profound liberating changes in our lives.

Both of these aspects of a contemplative in action show a committed love, but some people are called to emphasize one more than the other. The second aspect, more suitable for the pastoral ministry, although it does not absolutely exclude other forms of commitment, is the form of militancy adopted by Jesus himself and the apostles. They renounced power and political partisanship, and turned their attention to progressive liberation from all forms of oppression.

When Jesus and the apostles made known the presence of God in every human being, and the dignity of everyone, they declared their contemplative stand for the future of humanity. As well as this they gave a socio-political content to their contemplative vision by prophetically condemning the prevailing social and religious attitudes to human beings. Jesus showed a special love of those who were in need. This is not only a contemplative act, says Galilea but a social and political action in that it strives to liberate the poor from the oppression of unjust structures.

When Jesus proclaimed the beatitudes, it was impossible to announce and to live this message without living in hope, without being a contemplative. For contemplatives, the beatitudes are their ethical code, and thus the contemplative lives a prophecy which questions contemporary society. So the evangelical message from Elijah to Jesus gives us both views of the contemplative commitment to liberation. When looking at Jesus the contemplation of the Christian becomes eschatological; saving and transforming humanity and society from within. This implies changes in society, just as the liberation of Elijah implied a hope in the future and in the eschatological vocation of Israel.

Both the figures of Elijah and Jesus became archetypes having a contemplative message — and all Christians are called to live these to a greater or lesser degree according to their function and calling in the Church and society. They bring together mysticism and commitment in the same contemplative vocation: to experience Jesus in prayer and in our neighbor, especially those in need.

Jesus and Prayer

Galilea notes that the following of Jesus is revealed to us as a gift from God. This gift grows in us by the contemplative dimension of the Christian life and the way we pray. The gift of God comes to us in a special way in prayer, in which we put on Christ. Prayer communicates to us the experience of Jesus, a contemplative experience which is necessary for our fidelity. In prayer we fathom the depths of what it means to follow him in contemplative prayer, leading us to the Father, Son and Spirit.

Prayer is also inseparable from the following of Jesus because of the motivation behind it. What gives quality to any commitment are the motives which inspire it. In all Christian spirituality, and especially Carmelite spirituality, our motivation comes from the Word of Jesus and not from ideologies. When we personally experience Jesus we develop the motives for our mission.

Fr. Galilea says that there are some in today's world, and even some Christians, who ask if prayer still has any relevance. This is more pressing a question as the world becomes more secularized and technology takes over so many functions of our daily life. Some are tempted to see prayer as an evasion of responsibility to protect the environment and bring technology into the service of people. Others think that prayer reinforces a dualism in our daily lives and our religious lives — like encountering God in prayer as opposed to encountering God in the service of human beings — a dualism which many do not hold in today's Church.

Any principles which seek to answer these questions of some modern Christians would assume that the *way* we pray changes, although prayer itself has a permanent value in Christian spirituality. The way we pray changes not only with eras, but with different cultures and different times in our life. We need to adapt constantly our way of praying and integrate it to the demands of our day-to-day lives.

For Fr. Galilea the first principle in our need for adaptation is to recongnize that Jesus prayed and was known as a person of prayer. This prayer was and is for the renewal of humankind and influences what neither technology nor ideology can influence: sin, freedom, faith, love and resurrection. When we pray we pray the prayer of Jesus and he prays in and through us. God wants us to join with him in the renewal of the universe and the liberation of all men and women.

The second fundamental principle in understanding Christian prayer, according to Galilea is the belief that our God is a personal God who speaks, listens, and communicates with us, and with whom we can have a relationship as we can with any other person. The God of revelation, the Father of Jesus Christ is not a philosophical proposition, but a real person who has decided to enter our history in order to invite us to participate in his life, to listen to us and to act in us and through us. Prayer is, for the person of faith, a response to God's call, a need of love, a need to dialogue and become friend in the sharing in salvation.

The third fundamental principle in appreciating Christian prayer is to realize that people, by their very nature and by the seed implanted by baptism, are called to get to know God. We can certainly meet God through mediations, like our neighbor, our work and events of our daily lives. However, we are also called to meet God as he is, to contemplate him as he is as a person who loves us, and wants to be with us. If we deny this call to contemplation we will be incomplete human beings, just as St. Augustine realized that our hearts are made for God and will not rest until they rest in him. Even with the darkness of faith we can meet God "face to face" as St. John of the Cross said. The manner in which we meet God in prayer is on a different level than that of other encounters (neighbor, etc.) and we cannot refuse it without diminishing our own development and destiny. At the same time, prayer is our guarantee that we will really discover Christ in our neighbor, the events of our lives and of our society.

The ability to find Christ in others does not come from our own psychological resources or ideological motivations, but rather from our contact with God in prayer, the fruit of faith nourished by prayer, and the urgings of the Spirit of Christ living and acting in our hearts. While contemplatives are called to use technology, statistics and all the human knowledge and resources at their disposal and to put them at the service of people, their inner motivation comes from Christ, his grace and his Spirit. There is no competition here, but a collaboration between a gracious God, people and all creation working together to liberate men and women both interiorly and from exterior oppression.

From this we see the need of basing our prayer on firm convictions, rooted in faith. Often, if our need for prayer is merely a psychological need, we will be tempted to abandon its practice and claim a lack of time. But when we come up against the difficulties of our interior life and of the apostolate, we will realize that we need special graces from Christ. However, there are great helps that come to us only from Jesus in prayer. It is here, in an encounter with Jesus renewed each day, that we develop a oneness with God to see things in the light of the heart of the Gospel. The lack of prayer in our lives, if it is culpable and habitual, leads us into a sort of spiritual and apostolic anemia with the accompanying powerlessness to remain faithful to all the demands of the Gospel.

A final fundamental principle of Christian prayer is, Fr. Galilea believes, that it is an answer to God's initiative — a God who reaches out to us. It is not people who take the initiative in prayer; but there is a supernatural element to it. God calls us first and we answer him. Christianity is, above all, a religion of a God who seeks out people, a God who takes the initiative in sheer love, to liberate them, and to share a life with him.

Galilea says that the liturgy, the teacher of prayer, by its very structure, embodies this mystery of call and response. In the prayer songs, readings, silences of the liturgy of the Word, there is a response of human beings to the Word of God spoken to them. This structure of the liturgy reveals the basic meaning of Christian prayer.

Based on these principles, Galilea contends that Christian prayer has its own anthropology. It follows the physical, emotional, social and spiritual exigencies of the human person. This Christian anthropology of prayer has often been forgotten, both in liturgical prayer and in private prayer. We have to remember that it is the whole person who relates to God, and so we have to use our culture, art, history in all the signs and symbols of prayer. The affective side of a person, the vocal expressions which nourish prayer, the age of the person, the stage of their faith and intellectual development must all be taken into account when conducting the liturgy and helping people to pray.

Therefore, the problem of prayer in our modern world is very much related to the way we live our life. Each Christian needs to establish an inner discipline in their lifestyle, in order to have the freedom for the authentic contemplative dialogue with God — the destiny of all Christians. Some have the daily

Eucharist and Prayer of the Hours to nourish them, some have time for daily reading of the Scriptures, some choose a quiet time in each day for reflection, while others concentrate on their breathing and posture in silence. Whatever one chooses, one needs to introduce a certain discipine to have a daily contemplative encounter with the Lord.

This anthropology of prayer needs to take into account what we used to call "distractions." What is important is the work of the Holy Spirit working in us. So called distractions have to do with the affective side of our nature, and during times of distraction many things come to mind which help us to know ourselves better. Galilea suggests that what we call distractions may help us to discover our motives, and those people and events which are really concerning us. Many spiritual writers have recommended that we quietly hand over our "distractions" to Jesus as part of our prayer.

Finally, Christian prayer is the prayer of the Church. This means that Christians never really pray alone, even when praying by themselves; they pray as part of a whole, which is the Church, always in union with people, and always "with the Church," and celebrating the sacraments.

These principles and reflections on Christian prayer enunciated by Fr. Galilea, a great lover of the Carmelite tradition, lead to a redefinition of the Christian contemplative. Contemplation is not a dualistic notion present in some of the traditions of the Church; it is not fidelity to practices and methods of prayer. The contemplative in today's world is one who has an experience of God, who is capable of meeting God in history, in the social system, in our brothers and sisters, and through prayer. As Karl Rahner says you will not be able to be a Christian in the modern world without being a contemplative, and you cannot be a contemplative without having an experience of Christ and his kingdom in history. In this sense, Christian contemplation will guarantee the survival of the faith in a secularized and political world of the future.

A Carmelite Synthesis

Carmelites of today, in dialogue with the Spirit of the Lord in the Word of God, listening to the call of the Church of today, and attentive to the cry of the poor and powerless, are called to renew their tradition and spirituality. They have something to offer today's world, and men and women of the now have much to offer the Carmelites. For centuries Carmelites have faced the challenge to live faithfully their tradition of the call to contemplation and mysticism in every epoch of history. No matter how successful, they can report to people that the struggle is worthwhile.

Among the elements of contemporary theology, the theology of liberation seems to dialogue well with the Carmelite tradition.

Many of our people live and are working in countries where there are extremes between the rich few and the poor majority. In countries like Latin America, Africa, the Philippines, for example, conferences of bishops, theologians and local Church people talk in terms of liberation. They say that it is the Church's duty to help liberate people from poverty and injustices. The Carmelite tradition is challenged to enter into dialogue with this kind of thinking and help develop a spirituality applicable to this context.

In summary, the Carmelite tradition offers a spirituality of personal and interior liberation. This requires first and foremost a commitment to Jesus, his person and his message which can give men and women the only true liberation. The Gospel of Jesus calls men and women to use Gospel values in order to create a new heaven, a new earth, and so become the new creation.

Second, to liberate, we must be liberated. This means that we must be continually concerned about being free from our own inner idols before we can free people of injustices and poverty. Without a parallel concern for inner conversion, our efforts at social liberation will be in jeopardy.

This can be seen by the early pilgrim-hermits on Mount Carmel who were free of the entanglements of Church and society. We can learn this also from St. Teresa and St. John who would have us abandon all ambitions so as to be free not only for Jesus, but for our neighbor. Their language can be quite easily adapted into the more contemporary language of liberation, and some of our writers see them as great supporters of a liberation spirituality.

This gets support not only from the Spanish mystics, but from our 20th century saints, like Blessed Titus and Blessed Teresa Benedict (Edith Stein). These have shown that martyrdom is the ultimate liberation. This prospect is facing many of our men and women praying and working in those contexts. Thus, the spirituality of martyrdom had been emphasized in this century in the Carmelite tradition. This gained support from St. Teresa who saw martyrdom as a grace that comes from a life of daily abnegation and love — and cannot be fabricated or improvised.

Another element in the spirituality of liberation is a radical poverty. This implies both a simplicity of lifestyle, but also a poverty of spirit in the sense of a detachment from prestige, honors and positions. St. Teresa supports this. She sees poverty as freeing us for service — not so much free from this and that — but freeing us for.

The God-question

Today the theological discussion of liberation also raises the God question. What kind of God do we follow? What is the authentic God of revelation? Who is the Father of the Jesus of the Gospels — the Jesus we have committed ourselves to?

This too is a matter for our personal and inner liberation — we need to abandon any imperfect notion of God and convert ourselves to the one, true God — the one who cannot be manipulated, nor domesticated, nor the one who will allow us to remain comfortable and cosy. We are called to the God who challenges us to conversion, flexibility and creativity, the God of mercy, justice and solidarity. Only if we believe in and follow this God will our spirituality develop our commitment to peace and justice in the world. St. John of the Cross is someone in our tradition who liberates God. He teaches us to let God be God, and to allow God to mould us according to his Spirit. Since there can be no liberation without our liberating ourselves from false notions of God, the Carmelite tradition has much to say to liberation theology in the spirit of humble dialogue. John's Dark Night is the itinerary which helps us find God without deforming him. In John's spiritual synthesis, we liberate God from our imperfect ways of believing in him and our imperfect ways of loving him.

One of the difficulties of understanding St. John of the Cross today stems from his poetic language. One concept which may help translate St. John to the contemporary Church is the notion of our inner liberation from false notions of God. This will lead us to a clearer understanding of his symbols of night and nothingness. We can also take his notions of solitude, desert and retreat and adapt them to modern spirituality which sees the need for quiet reflection, alone with God. The desert is a form of liberation, as St. Thérèse understood, because it forces us to face the truth about ourselves, our lives and our relationships. In the desert and retreat we are stripped of all our illusions about ourselves — we are set free.

Carmelite Spirituality

Carmelite spirituality can help modern people to step aside and reflect. Busy people are often oppressed with the deceptions of mass media, consumerism and passing pleasures. These people can be helped in their search for freedom for a life close to Jesus and service of those in need.

Finally, Carmelite spirituality can help people to pray. These are a series of constants in the tradition of Carmelite prayer. They are:

1. *The practice of the presence of God.*
2. *The immersion in the mystery of God, which means prayer — a gift from God.*
3. *A prophetic awareness of the Word of God as found in Scripture and the signs of the times.*
4. *An immersion in Sacred Scripture — as a nourishment of prayer.*
5. *A firm anchoring in the liturgical prayer of the Church.*
6. *A prayer which blends the intellectual and affective dimensions of dialogue with God, but with a stress on the affective side, which is comfortable with both western and eastern influences.*
7. *Prayer considered as an anticipation of our activity in the eschaton.*
8. *We take Mary as the beloved model of contemplative prayer.*

For the Carmelite today contemplation is the experience of God in all the dimensions of human life — experiencing God both transcendent and incarnate. The contemplative hears the Word of God in the cry of the poor, in the voice of the Church (the community of the disciples of Jesus). The contemplative is one who has an experience of Jesus in the Paschal Mystery — in a succession of deaths and resurrections which form a spirituality of change. This Jesus continues to set free from all that prevents us from rising — he lifts us up to follow him on risky unknown paths. Part of the Paschal Mystery for the contemplative is that we gain our freedom when we are prepared to be identified with Jesus present in his little ones — the anawim.

Our song is Mary's Magnificat.

If you want a summary of this book, I would say Carmelites are:

PILGRIMS
POETS
and
PROPHETS.

For reflection: individuals or groups

1. How do you integrate your commitment to the world and your ministry with your prayer life?

2. How do you react when you read that you are called to be a mystic or a contemplative? How do you live this call to holiness?

3. What areas of learning do you need to undertake to follow the path that Jesus points out to you?

4. How is your spiritual journey a liberating experience for you? Write about a genuinely liberating experience that is important in your life?

Hints for writing and sharing:

See the end of the introduction

References used in Chapter 9

Documents of the Carmelite Order: *Towards a Prophetic Brotherhood.* Carmelite Center, Melbourne, 1984.

Council of the Provinces: *Justice and Peace.* Carmelite Communications Center, Melbourne, 1984.

Blanchard, D., O.Carm. (Ed.) "Liberation Spirituality: Carmelite Perspectives." *Sword* 47 (1987), Nos. 1 and 2.

Galilea, S., *Following Jesus.* Orbis Books, Maryknoll, NY, 1981.

ST PAULS

This book was designed and published by St. Pauls/Alba House, the publishing arm of the Society of St. Paul, an international religious congregation of priests and brothers dedicated to serving the Church through the communications media. For information regarding this and associated ministries of the Pauline Family of Congregations, write to the Vocation Director, Society of St. Paul, 7050 Pinehurst, Dearborn, Michigan 48126. Phone (313) 582-3798 or check our internet site, www.albahouse.org